FLAWED MOM
too

BOOKS BY AMBER FARRAR

FLAWED MOM

FLAWED MOM too

A NONFICTION

AMBER FARRAR

Flawed Mom Too

This book is a work of nonfiction that is based on facts, real events, and real people. Names, characters, places, and incidents are the product of the authors' life stories.

Trade Paperback ISBN: 9781692343309

Copyright © 2019 Amber Farrar

Cover design by Amber Farrar

All rights reserved. No part of this book may be reproduced or transmitted in any form or by any means, electronic or mechanical, including photocopying and recording, or by any information storage and retrieval system, without permission in writing from the publisher.

Published in the United States by Phenomenal Daughters.

Names: Farrar, Amber, author.

Title: Flawed Mom Too: a nonfiction / Amber Farrar.

Description: Includes bibliographical references and index.

Identifiers: ISBN: 9781692343309 (softcover)

Categories: Self-Help / Motivational and Inspirational / Biography and Autobiography / Personal Memoirs.

Printed in the United States of America

2019

DEDICATION

For

My bonus dad, Roderick Pratt, I love you forever. Thank you for all of your love, support, and hard work that you poured into the Flawed Mom brand.

My great-granny, Margaret Levy, I am grateful for your part in my journey. Your class, sharpness, and ability to light up any room will live in me forever.

My entire family, especially my mom and daughters, thank you so much for your love and inspiration.

And for Flawed Moms who live and love trapped by stereotypical roles and expectations.

Dear Heavenly Father,

      I love You. I respect You. I come to You as humble as I know how. I trust You at all times, in every area of my life. I lean on You for help in all things. I thank You for orchestrating everything to strengthen me for what You had planned for me, Flawed Mom Too. I am grateful to You for connecting Flawed Mom Too authors and allowing us to be influential in the lives of others. You are carrying our writings around the world. I know You are good. I have confidence in You. I know that You hear my prayer.

      I ask that You continue to bless all flawed moms beyond our expectations, keep your hands on us constantly, and overflow in our lives. Please help us to raise our children to love and to grow into their greatness. I ask that You help us to become parents with patience, and to model values: respect, trust, empathy, fairness, gratitude, integrity, determination, responsibility, and compassion. I ask that You continue to lead us to do.

Amen,

Your daughter, Amber

CONTENTS

	PRAYER	PG 4
1.	THE FLAWED MOM AMBER FARRAR	PG 8
2.	THE STUDENT MOM CLARISSA FUSE-HEMPHILL LAMETRIA S. JOHNSON	PG 17
3.	THE FIRST TIME MOM AMBER FARRAR	PG 43
4.	THE TEEN MOM JAMINA BEAL NICOLE TUCKER-COLEMAN	PG 53
5.	THE STAY AT HOME MOM MICAI EASLEY	PG 77
6.	THE NEW WIFE SWAYZE POLK	PG 88
7.	THE ENTREPRENEUR MOM DIANA BONNER AMBER FARRAR	PG 98
8.	THE GRIEVING MOM CHINARA MEEKS	PG 110
9.	THE SINGLE MOM PASSION BRAGG ROLANDA CREWS	PG 119
10.	THE STEPMOM SWAYZE POLK	PG 130

11. THE BATTLING DEPRESSION MOM   PG 133
    SHERIDA L. WILLIAMS
    CLOSING LETTERS   PG 142
    MAHOGANIE BRYANT
    DEMEISHA OWENS

ACKNOWLEDGMENTS

I would like to acknowledge flawed moms who played a role in the collaboration of Flawed Mom Too. This book would not be possible without your willingness to connect with me and to share your personal life experiences.

Most importantly, I wish to thank my mom, Yolanda, who provided patience, advice and guidance; my bonus dad, Roderick Pratt, who has supported and guided me through everything business related; my brother, Kaleb; my husband, DeMarco; and my five children, Amir, Dakai, Diya, Dumia and Dalyn, who supported me with love and understanding. Without you, I could never have reached this current level of power within.

1 THE FLAWED MOM

Most flawed moms want to explore, travel and cruise the world. Some like being able to say that they have been in or through different cities or try to seem better than others. Then there are flawed moms who have confidence and success, and like telling a good story.

I know flawed moms who never leave, stay in their communities and hometowns, which is their choice and okay. Stop worrying about what people think. Concentrate on what is best for you and your family.

While there is a desire to move to better places, the reality is every flawed mom does not have the ability to seek out living in a different state for whatever reason. There is a stigma associated with them not leaving: Women with children are more likely than men to live and raise their families in poverty, and face issues of low-paying work, gender wage gap, poor social safety net, lack of affordable child and health care, family caretaking, and responsibilities.

More often than not, flawed moms travel and/or relocate, and pursue improved homes and economic opportunities. We take a much-needed vacation or seek a better life for our families. We experience the world.

Often, I am asked, by other moms, "How do you make moves without a doubt?" The answer, "I trust God."

On June 9, 2017, my family of seven moved from St. Louis, MO to Houston, TX. I accomplished so much in one day, and will never forget letting myself be instead of pushing to get the move done. I accepted the moment and trusted everything is good. My heart longed for opportunities to grow and learn with my family in a different city. We needed something different.

On the day before move, I rented a truck, and then drove to my rental home to meet my cousin and DeMarco's, my fiancé at the time, brother. They helped me pack the truck as much as they could while DeMarco worked his normal employment hours. When they left, I continued to pack with the help of my kids.

DeMarco never wanted to leave St. Louis. He complained to me, and tried to find every excuse to avoid helping me to pack. I explained to him right then and there that nothing on earth would stop me from getting my belongings on the truck and moving to Houston the next day.

With that being said and understood, for that moment, DeMarco began to help. He, the children, and I did not finish packing that night; however, we did complete a lot and had little left to do on the next morning.

On the move day, I picked up a close friend, who helped drive my family and me to Houston. We rolled out. Same day, my children and I moved out of a rental home in St. Louis and into an apartment in Houston. I never thought twice about my decision to relocate or looked back on what I left behind.

I was five months pregnant with my fifth child, and had to adjust to life in a new city. Everyone, but me, looked at the move as a challenge. I considered it a change and accepted it with a positive attitude. My children and I were comfortable in our new environment.

Houston was a city that I had visited only for weekends. Now, it was where I would raise my children. I took the initiative to learn about different settings, the best school districts, and hidden gems to explore with my children.

How much money was available to my children and me? Not much for a long time. I have a great seasonal job. Tax season is busy for me as a tax preparer. I assemble tax returns for a period of three and a half months. The job affords me an opportunity to live comfortably as a stay-at-home mom, one of the best decisions of my life.

DeMarco resided and worked in St. Louis for a month after my move to Houston, which was okay with me. He and I decided it would benefit us in the months to come. We avoided societal pressures that could make engaged couples feel like they are not winning if they live separately in different cities, especially if the woman is pregnant.

Two and a half weeks later, and six months pregnant, I drove my children and me from Houston to St. Louis for DeMarco and my wedding ceremony. The 13-hour drive, really more due to food and breaks, was enjoyable with my children. We were excited to see our family and close friends.

However, once in St. Louis, I wanted to leave badly. Was it wedding stress while pregnant? I don't know. I just wanted the weekend to be over. Several times I asked, "Can we leave now and go back to Houston?"

On July 1, 2017, DeMarco and I were married. I insisted on driving to Houston that same evening, but waited until the next day. Neither DeMarco nor the children were ready to return. They wanted to spend more time with our families, who poured so much love into us during our stay in St. Louis.

DeMarco stayed in Houston for a few days, and then returned to St. Louis for work. He had a few weeks before his resignation date.

The last three months of pregnancy, I was faced with difficulties and ended up in the emergency room a few times. I had intense and throbbing head pains. It was discovered that my issue was wisdom tooth pain. If you have ever experienced the pain, you know it is worse than childbirth. I asked myself, "Why would this happen to me all of a sudden, while pregnant with four children in a new city?" I did not undergo a tooth distraction during my pregnancy and stayed in pain.

A month after the move to Houston, my truck was stolen. One morning, I woke up to go to a doctor's appointment and my truck was not where I parked it. I called DeMarco, who decided to come immediately to Houston. Same conversation, we argued and he decided not to come at all. At the time, DeMarco and I were not on good terms. A day passed and we were still going back and forth on the phone. On that day, he decided to come to Houston.

After a few weeks of marriage, DeMarco and I did not know if we wanted to stay married. We did not know what we were doing. I wondered, "Why would the first month of marriage be the hardest?"

On top of that, my children started giving me the blues about our move to Houston. Now, I am the only one excited about the move. Every single day, they shared and I listen to their desire to go permanently back to St. Louis. I did not foresee the consequences.

Eventually, I found the energy to leave the apartment and ignore them. I knew that my intentions were good, and my decision to relocate the family was for a better life.

All of my children are very talented, and I knew that DeMarco would make good money and have fewer distractions. However, they complained and said that I was the only one who wanted to move. DeMarco said, "You are being selfish by making the children stay here in Houston." No one, but me, saw the big picture vision.

In St. Louis, DeMarco, my children and I were living in our comfort zone. I wanted us to discover new opportunities and life goals. I wanted to make changes so we would reach our full potential and abilities every day. Moving to Houston meant choosing to be happy and more grateful. You cannot live your best life operating like there is a battery in your back. There are times that you have to be uncomfortable.

If things did not work out in Houston, I would have had no problem moving back to St. Louis. I stayed prepared to go backward to move forward. However, I am very optimistic and make things happen. Always, I give things a try.

My family and I have experienced our share of extreme weather, but nothing like Hurricane Harvey in August 2017. It will never leave my memory. There were many lessons learned. I was scared. Yet, I did now want to leave Houston and go back to St. Louis. DeMarco asked, "Do you want to leave?" Then stated, "We have to go now before it gets bad, and we can't."

I stood on my decision to stay, and knew we would be good. I did not want to go into my savings to support our living in St. Louis and in Houston. So we stayed and the next three weeks we were trapped in our apartment together. The entire city was under water for that period.

We knew the hurricane was going to happen, and were prepared with perishable items, but not mentally. I thank God we survived. One of my cousins was rescued by boat from her flooded home. She stayed with us.

Hurricane Harvey took lives, homes and businesses. It was the worst thing that happened in the midst of me trying to convince my family that is move was right for us.

I listened to them go on and on for another year, and still did not fold. As I stated before, "My intentions were good." I would never do anything to put my family in a situation that is not healthy nor beneficial.

Everything about being in Houston was different. In St. Louis, my doctor told me that I could have a vaginal birth. Though in Houston, doctors do not believe in doing a vaginal birth after cesarean. So my last childbirth would be a cesarean. I had one ten years prior. I am very scared of surgeries. After hearing the delivery details, I had high blood pressure for the remainder of my pregnancy.

When I arrived in Houston, doctors did not want to see me as a patient because I was six months pregnant. I should have considered waiting to move until the baby was born. I left soon as the school year ended in St. Louis.

Finally, a doctor in Chinatown, neighborhood in Houston, was going to see me. Imagine being a girl from North St. Louis City and putting your life in the hands of a foreign doctor. On top of driving to a clinic and eying Chinese-only business signs all around the community. Everything, except street signs and a few American restaurants, was in Chinese lettering. I was feeling all the way out of place. Some days, depending on the area of town, I still have the same emotion. Still nothing is making me want to leave. I am finding interest and importance in everything that has to do with my move.

My cesarean delivery was planned ahead of time because I developed pregnancy complications and had a previous cesarean. The thought of the procedure had me nervous for over three months. My mom would come from St. Louis to take care of responsibilities with my other children.

On October 13, DeMarco and I drove three minutes to the hospital from hour apartment. He tried to keep me calm, along with the doctor. Both looked at my face and knew I was uneasy about the surgery, and talked to me during the preparation for delivery. At 2pm, I had my fifth child, Dalyn Anthony Farrar, in Houston.

My mom arrived from St. Louis to take care of responsibilities with my other children. She had picked them up from school. They waited patiently in the designated hospital area to see the newest member of our family.

The 2018-2019 school year was my children's second academic experience in Houston. It took that long for them and DeMarco to adjust. Thank you, God. No more hearing about how much they hated the decision to relocate.

Technology was our source for breaking news and latest stories in St. Louis. Too, social media was good for sharing information, memories, and keeping up with family recent happenings. We read about so much violent crime in the north city of St. Louis and in the Greater St. Louis area, and wanted no parts of witnessing and living around it. For that reason, I did not want to visit St. Louis. Since we moved to Houston, I returned to St. Louis three times and only one time was planned.

My daughters wrote their first book in April 2018. My family and I returned in August 2018 for their book signing. Too, the girls participated as vendors at The Back to School Community Empowerment Festival. In March 2019, my bonus dad passed away, and April 2019, my great-grandmother transitioned. We returned for both funeral services.

My mom has visited Houston more times than I expected. I am very thankful that she has been in my corner through any and everything. She has not missed a graduation, awards ceremony, childbirth or anything important to my family. Her support mattered more than anything.

My husband was not always mentally supportive during my transition. However, he was present and helped in his best possible way.

Having or not having money did not have an influence on my decision to relocate. I am going to take every opportunity to earn it, no matter where I reside. Love is what you need. I completely understand people being hesitant to move, especially with children and possibly no support. My children made me feel like I was ruining their lives and setting them up for failure. I was exposing them to a better living situation.

When single moms ask me for my thoughts on relocating, I have my own story to tell. Everyone is uniquely different, and so are his or her experiences. All I can do is encourage them to try a new situation. I refuse to give a person, especially a woman, a false sense of belonging and hope. We are let down enough. The difference between successful and unsuccessful people is mindset.

Your friends who have been around for a long time are not the only people willing to support you. Friends who have been around for a short while are encouraging too. I have met parents at my children's school and extracurricular activities who have similarities and differences. We communicate and connect beyond my expectations.

Now that the stubbornness has worn off my children, they give support in our learning and developing in Houston. Yet, sometimes my children are on board and other times they are off board. One week they are vegan, and the next week they are caught with a chicken sandwich and chees fries. Still, I take everything that they say into consideration. Ultimately, a life changing decision has to be made by an adult. Children do not like change too much. If you are thinking about moving them from their family and friends, do not expect for them to be your biggest supporters.

My old boss told me, "Excuses are monuments of nothingness. They build bridges to nowhere. Those who use these tools of incompetence seldom become nothing and are worthy of nothing."

Amber Farrar

2 THE STUDENT MOM

As I'm contemplating going back to college to earn a degree, after an 11-year break, my head is filled with every negative thought you could imagine. "I'm too old," and "It'll rip my pockets apart." I assumed it would be challenging, and believed it would not allow enough time for school, work, and family. I am worrying and letting my negative thoughts talk me out of starting my journey as a college student again. This is just the start of my journey as a student mom.

I grew up in north city of St. Louis. I come from a neighborhood of violence with no role models. We never talked about going to college; we were too busy surviving gun violence.

As a kid, I always wanted a different life for my future children. Advancing my education was never my goal. Yet, I always wanted more, but didn't know how to take the steps forward.

After having my second daughter, I wanted to be a strong role model for both of them and further my education by earning a college degree. Doing this, I would have accomplished something that no one can ever take from me.

When I graduated from high school, I enrolled in college with no resources, no plan, no goal, and no motivation. I just knew that going to college was supposed to be the right thing to do after high school. My parents never encouraged me to go.

Both of my parents experienced the loss of their mother and father at an early age. My father was age three, and my mother was age six. They had no mother figure to pour into them and their development.

My father, Clarence, dropped out of high school, and

my mother, Fannie, dropped out of medical school for her own reasons. She allowed fear to steal her dream of becoming a nurse. My parents encouraged me the best way they knew and that was to stay out the streets.

There are many things that my parents didn't know about me. I enrolled in St. Louis Community College-Forest Park directly out of high school. However, I didn't take my college education or anything seriously.

I was too busy working a full-time job and paying rent and utilities at my apartment. My school schedule was starting to weigh heavily on my personal life, as working and spending my paychecks on bills and material things became key to me. Creating and maintaining the best work, school, and life balance was challenging. Just going to school, work, and then party at the clubs was routine stress.

The pressure started to take a toll on my body and grades. I received failing grades, which caused a low GPA. I made the ultimate decision and dropped out of college after attending for two and a half semesters.

Shortly afterward, I became pregnant with my first child due to free time on my schedule. After my first child, Summer, was born, I had no desire to attend college again. I was busy being a new mother and adjusting to my new normal.

I worked very hard, kept a good job, and felt like I was doing everything right. But, I was still missing something. Everything I wanted to do (start a business, further my education, and get my real estate license) was all on the other side of fear. I allowed the negativity from my environment to seep into me, and discourage me from my dreams.

It was something about motherhood that motivated me

to want more for my life so I could pour into my children. Going back to school would always visit my mental, but I'd immediately dismiss the thoughts with my negative thinking and doubting myself.

After having my second child, Dreem, I realized enough was enough. I needed to make changes that would be a positive impact on my life.

When Dreem was six months, I enrolled in real estate school. I was nervous and excited. I attended school tired from being up all night, breastfeeding, and not focusing entirely. Eventually, I concentrated enough and passed out of the class. I moved to the next step to have the opportunity to take my national exam. I failed and immediately shut down. I realized that the timing wasn't right, and I didn't have proper childcare in order. I was sleep-deprived and drained mentally. I didn't believe I could do it, so I wasn't successful.

Once again, thoughts crossed my mind about school, but I felt as if I couldn't do it. My husband Wesley tried to encourage me to study harder and retake the exam, but I started a full-time job instead. It was the same job that I turned down a month prior because the pay was too low, and I was in real estate school. The employer caught me at a vulnerable time, and we agreed on a higher pay.

While working at my job, I knew life had more to offer me. At that moment, I wasn't losing anything but time. I felt foolish and dumb, and thought about where I would be in life if I'd stayed in college. I would be so much further in life. I realized that's not how life operates; it's not about the pretty fairy tale story. Sometimes you have to experience life, so you'll be grateful when an opportunity crosses your path.

When I first applied to Lindenwood University, my admission, scholarships, and grants were denied due to my low GPA. I was currently paying for my behavior from 11 years ago, which finally caught up with me. I had to write appeals and obtain letters of recommendation to help me get accepted at Lindenwood University. After I received my letter of acceptance, I was excited, but I decided to go back to the college I dropped out of 11 years ago.

I was accepted and excited about my new journey at St. Louis Community College-Forest Park. The price I paid for taking such a long break from school is I had to start over from scratch. My husband supported me to go back to school. I kept in mind and recalled his college journey and knew if I applied the same ambition as he did, I'd be fine.

Working and going to school can create a dilemma, and precisely that's what happened. I thought everything would flow smoothly because I informed my employer that I was about to pursue a college degree. I was denied the flexibility to go to school and work. My supervisor once told me, "Clarissa, you can't work and go to school. You need to choose one." I thought to myself, the audacity of them to tell me to choose between my livelihood and my future. Once again, I was writing letters to upper management for an opportunity to have a flexible schedule so I could do both.

I valued school and took advantage of the opportunity to learn new things and meet positive people. Never allow your past to determine your future. It was rough transitioning back to school, and having daughters that are six years apart with active schedules is a challenge in itself.

As a student mom, my entire day is consumed with

school life, work, or children. There is no time for play, and it's not fair to my children if all of my time is dedicated to school. So I planned our outings according to my school schedule and homework.

My oldest daughter Summer was in girl scouts, accelerated math programs, and afterschool programs, which all involved parent participation. Dreem was in swim lessons. My husband Wesley has a hectic entrepreneurship schedule. All our schedules were different, which made things complicated. Even though my husband is helpful, supportive, and very encouraging, and tries to take the weight off my shoulders with our daughters, I'm a very hands-on mom and stay involved with everything. LOL. I love to share all my daughters' childhood moments with them.

One of my new words became "NO," which caused me many sacrifices. I wasn't able to travel. Each year on my birthday I was in school, I wasn't able to attend events, parties, or gatherings. It was either have fun or do my homework. Since time doesn't wait for anyone, I had to focus on school. Throughout my journey in school, professors told me, "School is not created for minorities to succeed."

I have been exposed to drop out by more people than I could imagine. People told me to change my major in psychology because minorities struggle in this field. I realize people tried to instill their fears in me.

Purchasing books and paying for tuition is a hassle that was a new task my husband and I became accustomed too. The stress of being a full-time student, wife, mother, and full-time employee is already enough to make any sane person feel overwhelmed and stressed. When life starts kicking your ass, you start to evaluate and analyze your situation. I thought about dropping out of school several times because quitting is very easy. Leaving is only natural because it won't help you get anywhere far. However, I know anything in life that is worth having will be hard to get.

      I got used to being up all night doing homework, writing ten-page research papers, creating PowerPoint presentations, studying for exams, doing math that looked as if it was written in a foreign language, driving to school in rain, sleet or snow, being at school activities with my daughters, holiday parties for my daughters, going on field trips, cooking full course meals before and after school, grocery shopping, helping with homework, and the list goes on. My responsibilities were significant, but I wasn't going to allow anything to stop me from pursuing my college degree this time.

      My job eventually approved my request for a split schedule. The shift for work now was split for school and work after fighting for it. Remember a closed mouth doesn't get fed. It was finally approved by management a few months prior, at that moment, I became a target because I was the only employee taking an extended lunch break and going to school. This was now my routine for a couple of semesters. My professors couldn't believe I was at school on my lunch break, and I couldn't believe it either.

      I was doing everything in my power to attend college. On September 21, 2016, which is my youngest daughter Dreem's birthday, I had a flat tire on my way to school, which landed me my walking papers from my job. I returned to work four hours later than scheduled. I was terminated two days after and they said, "We told you that you couldn't do both, school and work, so we have to let you go." I was relieved and felt as if I could finally fully spread my wings. At that moment I made up my mind to never let a temporary job steal my dreams. That was the last time I would clock in at a job.

Things became rough financially, but I'm thankful for my husband's support. I continued my journey in my last semester of school. Before graduating, I had to attend three campuses within the same semester. I drove from the west to the north and city campuses all in one day for four days of the week, and took 17 credit hours. It was one of the most challenging semesters I had experienced before. I was attending school and now operating a new business.

What keeps me motivated between obstacles and barriers, the thought, "When shit gets hard, go harder." I have been recognized on the Dean's List several times, maintained a 3.5 GPA or higher, accepted in the Honor Society, and received professor compliments. After countless emotional nights, I graduated with my associate's degree in business on May 20, 2017. It was one of the most deserving days. I felt so many emotions because just the thought of how long it took me mentally to build myself up was a blessing.

My husband, daughters and family were excited to see all my hard work paid off. The look on my daughters' faces during my graduation was worth all of my sleepless nights. I wished my parents were there to see me too. Some people may think an associate's degree, that's all you have. But, you should always clap for the next person regardless of what stage of life they may be in. The beginning stage is the hardest. That's when you experience the majority of your emotions. It doesn't matter if a person has a GED or a PhD both is an accomplishment.

I passed my real estate exam, received my Missouri Real Estate license, and started a few businesses. Rich Tax Services was my first one. My husband and I purchased a few investment properties, and I enrolled in an undergraduate degree program-major in Psychology-at the University of Missouri-St. Louis.

Never let anyone tell you something is impossible. Show them it is possible. When you have a dream, your vision becomes apparent, which will lead you to your destiny. My job told me that it was impossible to work and go to school. When I departed from my employer, I did more.

In my free time, I connect and speak with other individuals who appear to be weak-minded to the wrong crowd. I encourage them to follow their dreams and set attainable goals, so they don't become discouraged.

I committed myself to start and never stop. My daughters Summer and Dreem are my motivation, and I'm their role model. I instilled the importance of education into them at a young age. They attended AAA school districts. Both are scholars. Summer is an ongoing honor student and Dreem admires learning. They discuss going to college, which I led by example. My goal is to accomplish something that can never be taken away from me, which is my college degree.

Now, I volunteer in different communities to help plant in community gardens so people can have fresh fruits and vegetables, at abuse shelters for women and their children to encourage them to never get discouraged due to hardships, and with Girl Scouts to promote self-awareness and problem-solving, and to inspire girls to manage themselves and resolve conflict. I push hard, and give motivational speeches.

I understood that I could be a better person for my daughters and myself. When I obtained my bachelor's degree, it was the effort, hard work, dedication, and motivation that I'm most proud of.

Going through a challenging time in my life, I've endured genuine people that supported my journey. I've been in contact with knowledgeable, like-minded, positive individuals. My husband, my mother, and a few others were very helpful along my school journey.

When you have a college degree, you can pursue better-paying careers, provide for your family, and be the motivation for other individuals that want to accomplish the same goals.

Being an entrepreneur and full-time student are two pieces of my puzzle, the story of my life, and I love it. My college degree is my backup plan. Being a first-generation college student is rough, but following your dreams is a great satisfaction. I now believe in me and believe anything is possible with faith, determination, hard work and consistency, and patience.
My advice for parents in college:

1. Have a clear and level mind.
2. Identify your needs and choose the right college.
3. Schedule a time to interview an advisor.
4. Choose a major based on your interests, values, passions, and abilities (helps to complete assignments).
5. Have adequate childcare in place.
6. Have reliable transportation.
7. Select a commuter college.
8. Get a planner (they're beneficial).

9. Buy your books and school supplies.
10. Print out your entire Syllabus.
11. Introduce yourself to your professor, and explain your goal for the class.
12. Keep open communication with your professors.
13. Get a tutor (if needed).
14. Set time aside for school life (homework).
15. Learn to say, "NO" (to anyone, even a good friend; don't feel bad about it).
16. Select your school schedule early to ensure classes of your choice.
17. Read professor reviews on "Rate My Professor."
18. Block out negative energy and people.
19. Surround yourself around positive people.
20. Find and apply for scholarships and grants.
21. Have a financial plan (how can you work and attend school).
22. Give yourself a pat on the back. "You got this."

Follow these steps, and you'll have a successful school journey.

The moral of my story is: Keep moving forward because everyone doesn't want to see you succeed, and that's okay. Don't allow others to project their fears on you. You can detour, but never give up. Follow your passion and the money will follow you.

Clarissa Fuse-Hemphill

Where do you start and what do you do when you've agreed to be a co-author in a book when all you've ever done was write in a journal, more than 2-3 years ago? Do you give all you got or do you hold back until your big break? What if this is your big break? What if this is your season for God to move you closer to your destiny? What if the life that you've always dreamed of is still not a reality? What do you do? Well, I'll tell you. You put your big girl panties on and you give this opportunity everything you got. Holding back no punches.

Being a student mom isn't just about me going to college and obtaining any one, two, three or many degrees. It's about the life journey and decisions that I've made and continue to make.

You can go to school to better yourself and to obtain the status quo, which you've always dreamed of. But, what if life happens, and you find yourself having to redefine who and what you're fighting for? Do you continue to live and move just for you or do you begin to study each decision you make as if it's the last decision for the little people looking up to you?

My dream was to be married, 25 years old, and already graduated from 4-year college before starting a family. As you see, I said, "Starting a family," not just having children. I wanted this well-oiled, put-together life and marriage. I wanted to be well-established.

By whose standards was I measuring this up against? I don't know the answer to that question, but I do know that it broke me when it didn't add up. It broke everything in me to a level that I didn't see a way of putting the pieces back together. And, when I say, "I fought every second of the day to not be a statistic," it broke me even more when I realized that I was already a statistic.

Having completed high school, receiving my associate's degree, and completing one year of my Bachelor of Science degree, I thought I was on the best plan of my life. I thought I had it all together, but boy was I wrong.

Just when my life was moving forward, I began feeling that I was missing something and someone. And not necessarily a male companion, but missing the life that I cried out to God, "Save me from this life, and the people/world that don't love me back."

During all this missing, I didn't realize that I was missing my time with Jesus. My one-on-one with the true and living God that heard my cry, picked me up, washed me off, and forgave me for all the wrong that I had done. The one who didn't care if I wasn't meeting the status quo. The one who held me when I cried alone at night. The one who knew my past, but still promised me a favorable future.

And, just like a child whose parents were giving them all they can ask for, I still was finding myself intertwined in a world of mischief and foolishness. Seeking that which was not lost, I found myself not married, dating a man I didn't truly like or love, attending church every Sunday and Tuesday, and being pregnant at the age of 21.

Now don't get me wrong, I was 22 years old when I had my first son, and, in my book, I was uneducated. I hadn't at all learned all that there's to know about life or myself to be having a child. No degree or transcript, with my name on it, had prepared me for this journey.

To start with, I had not arrived at the place where I was financially stable to take care of a child and me. I had it all together for me, but what was I going to do about caring for a child? And, what about giving him some of the things he needed to thrive (time, stability, emotional support, structure)? I knew I didn't want him wanting for anything, especially when I was the child that spent my childhood watching the other children when the adults went out clubbing, attending school, or just hanging out at the house.

I was responsible for the children, so I knew what to do when they cried, how to change a diaper, and what TV shows they should or shouldn't watch. But, what I didn't know was that the child that I now had was going to be stuck with me for life.

Many of days, I would play with my son and accidentally call him, "Tee-Tee Baby," accidentally tell him, "Tee-Tee loves you," and then one day asked him, "When are your mommy and daddy coming to get you?"

The day I said that last one and realized what I had said, I knew that I had lost it. I knew that this thing was real, that this baby was mine and that I had to get it together so that I could become better prepared to take care of him. Not that I hadn't thought of all of this before, but life changes when you are holding that baby in your arms and he is depending on you to make it a better place. How do I make it all better when I've just messed it all up?

After having him, I felt like there was nothing left to give. The fight and tenacity that I once had were gone. The drive to be a successful businesswoman was no longer in my view. The fight to help others was screw them all.

How do you lose your fight and try to fight at the same time? This was just one of the many questions and thoughts running through my head when I looked into my son's big beautiful eyes. The other thoughts were voices of the people who told me that I had messed up and that my son's dad had messed my life up.

Everything was all good when he was emptying his pockets on me, driving me back and forth to college, expressing his love towards me every chance he got, and dealing with my terrible attitude. You never find out how people feel or think about you until you are no longer meeting their expectations.

It's hard to make a quick come back from feeling empty, but being the "seasoned" mom, I told my son's dad that we were going to make liars out of everybody and give our son the best of this world while leaving everybody in the dust while we do it. Feeling hurt and alone, even when my son's dad was right there the entire time, it wasn't easy. In my son's eyes, I made it look painless, for a period.

My son's dad and I agreed that we weren't going to send him to daycare until he could talk and tell us what was happening. So for the first two years of his life, I stayed home with our son, which was good because, at that time, I had no idea of where my life was going. I didn't know if or when I wanted to go back to work. However, I knew that I didn't want to go back and finish my bachelor's degree. The strong black woman in me said, "Girl you don't need the education to do what you want to do, so why go back and waste money."

I had no clue as to what I was going to do, but I did know that I wanted to get out of my momma house and show everyone who cared or didn't care that I still had it. It's so crazy because after doing everything that I could to not complete my bachelor's degree, I eventually ended up getting one. Let me back up and tell you all what I did beforehand.

Still trying to find myself and place my feet on solid ground, I was determined to be this all-mighty and all-powerful black woman. So, I enrolled in an apprenticeship program. This is where I learned the basics of carpentry and construction. I knew that I didn't want to do any of those jobs. But, I convinced myself that I was doing it to show my son that he can do anything he put his mind to, as well as to show people that I wasn't as bad off as they thought I was.

During the time apprenticing, I remember my Pastor asking me, "What are you doing?" I don't remember my response, but then and now I knew that she knew I was running. She did one of those God things, like ask a question that He already knows the answer to, but wants you to think about what you were doing. It's quite amusing, now, and some days I wonder where my life would be had I pursued a career in carpentry and construction?

When that was over, I decided to go to cosmetology school. Why, because I was still fighting myself not to finish my bachelor's degree. So, I told others and myself, a false truth, that I was going to cosmetology school because I wanted to one day own a salon and to know the business so that I could assure that the clients received top-notch services.

As I sat down with the advisor, she asked, "Why are you going to cosmetology school when you have only a year and a half left to complete your bachelor's degree?" I gave her the same answer as I gave other people. The look on her face let me know that she didn't believe me either.

I still wasn't thinking all the way clear, but at least I was back to thinking from a business standpoint, in my opinion. I enjoyed learning in the cosmetology world. I graduated, and passed both the written and practical exams. Heck, I even worked in a salon, for about two weeks.

During this time, my son spent most of his time at daycare, with his dad, or with my mom. I rarely saw him, and for me that was good. I thought that if I didn't see him, then I didn't have to face him and let him see the hurt, shame, and guilt in my eyes.

Searching and seeking for a way of escape is what I was doing while running in circles trying to outrun the idea of showing my son a defeated/flawed mom. I became the student mom of my life and baby when I say it knocked me down, but the God I serve had grace and mercy stored up and waiting on me.

God kept His promise to keep my son and I'll forever be grateful. I knew that I was messed up, and how I was thinking and living was not best for my son. So, I kept us in church and at the altar.

Getting back on my feet, mentally, wasn't easy because swallowing my pride and the pill of making pointless commitments was tearing me up more. So, what did I do? I gave my son and our future back to God.

After running from God, it was hard running back to Him, but I owed it to my son and myself to accept my faults and give it all back. God had brought me out before and I knew that He could do it again. Learning who I was and who God had ordained me to be, all over again, took time. But, in that time, I was able to show my son true love. What it meant and looked like to be committed to something and someone.

My son was able to see me grow and be healed. He saw me be broken, mistreated, and talked about. And, I still thanked and praised God for all that He had done.

Every struggle that I went through, during this time, my son, Elisha Johnson, went through it with me. He watched me feverously cry out to God for guidance. He watched me take needed time away for myself. And, although he didn't understand why he couldn't go, he still loved me when I returned.

During the time I reconnected with God, He took me back to a place of remembrance. And, and in that place, He reminded me that I had vowed to be the best example for my children and to never let anyone outshine me, and what I wanted to teach my children. So, I agreed to return to college and complete my bachelor's degree.

Completing this degree was not about me, but everything about Elisha and his siblings to come. I knew that I didn't want to have any unfinished things in my life that could give them the idea that they should leave things unfinished in their lives.

No matter what anyone else did I knew that the decisions and choices that I had made and will continue to make in life would be the ones that my children related to the most. Anybody else in their life could stop making moves, but I never and still don't want them to look at mommy and say, "Well you didn't finish." If I could press through all that I had been through and go through, then I have a strong foundation to stand on when I tell them, "The words can't and won't are not in our vocabulary."

On May 21, 2014, I walked across the stage and received my Bachelors of Science in Business Management degree from the University of Phoenix. The many days and nights of not being able to play with Elisha when he wanted to or taking him to the Science Center or Chuck E. Cheese just because was not worth it to me, but when he put his arms around me and said "Mommy I Love You," I balled like a baby.

I dedicated my bachelor's degree to my children and they will forever know that mommy did that one especially for them. I was no longer selfish, and never again will it be an option for me.

I had to grow up and accept the fact that my life was and is not my own. My children will forever be my driving force until the day that I'm done here, and I will forever fight me for them.

Still fighting to be the best, I knew there was more in me to give and do. So, I looked at the opportunities within my current job to help me be successful. Determined not to return to college I embarked on a leadership class at work. A year after graduating with my bachelor's degree, I completed the class with no advancement at the job.

Although completing the class didn't promise me any type of job advancements, I was hoping that it would give me the urge to go further within this company. Well, it didn't. And, it didn't even have me looking outside of the company because I knew if I looked, then I wouldn't be trusting God and the promises He's made over my life. As much as I didn't want to return to school I knew that I had to do something.

Luckily, God allowed me sit for a while (about 3 years). When that fire began to burn again, I knew it was nothing but God. During that time of sitting, God allowed me to go through and deal with things. If I would have been doing something else, I would not have been able to get through those obstacles. Before today, I didn't really realize that God had me sitting. But, as I write this chapter, I understand exactly what was going on. Now, four years after obtaining my bachelor's degree, I sometimes question myself, "Why didn't I just keep going or better yet, why didn't I know my true purpose?"

How do you live 30 plus years, have a child, know God and still not know your purpose? How? Well, my answer is that I did know my purpose. I knew and know what God has called me to do.

But, when you've felt like you've had to fight to be everything for everybody you tend to forget or not want to fight for yourself. You look at your life and assume that just because you've done so much and supported so many that someone would just wake up and be like "Here, I've started and mastered your dream for you now baste in it." LOL.

That's so not how life works, and God allowed me to have my little pity party until I got tired of waiting on the handouts that I really didn't want or need. According to my pastor, spoken during many of her teachings, "You can either be the one needing the help or the one giving the help – you choose." And yes, sometimes I want to be the one receiving the help, but oh how I enjoy the feeling of being the one giving the help.

Nothing boastful but just to know that God put something on the inside of you to help someone else reach their destiny or get over an obstacle is a feeling that's joyously indescribable. Being a servant is what I've learned this life is all about.

God is an amazing God and when He quickened my spirit to start moving again, I made sure to ask Him which way to go. Many opportunities came my way, but more schooling is what He wanted for me. When God has a plan for you it's for you and no matter how hard you fight it, if you truly love Him, you'll do it just the way He's orchestrated for you.

Summer 2018, I began the enrollment and registration process to return to school. I told as many people as I could so that I could continue with the courage to complete the process. Some people said, "More power to you," and "Congratulations." Others said, "I'll believe it when I see it." Now, the "I'll believe it when I see it" people were the ones that I agreed with. I couldn't believe that I was going back to school, especially when I found out all the legwork I had to do just to get accepted.

I questioned God and His decision because I just knew that if this was what He wanted me to do, then He would have already had the doors unlocked, opened, and my seat ready for me to sit in. But, I should have remembered that faith without works is dead and that if you're truly walking with God then it's a true faith walk.

So, by faith, I walked in that door and although, I was placed on academic probation, I was accepted into the program that God told me to apply for and in January 2019, I began work to obtain a master's degree in Professional Counseling at Lindenwood University. I was both excited and nervous, but still trusting God and His plan. A lot of people were shocked at the second-degree choice because it is totally opposite of the first degree, which I received 4 years ago. And, it was nowhere near the professional work I've been doing the last 18 years.

The first few weeks of school were a little trying because although I was familiar with being in college, I wasn't familiar with the psychology world. My background experience was business and health, but not psychology.

A shell shocker, I know. Once I got over my fears, a

little, and a good month or so into the program, I was beginning to see myself fully indulging into this new journey/chapter of my life. I began to see and understand the reasoning behind why God wanted me to go back to school versus being taught or mentored, by man (male or female).

A lot of transparency began to take place and I began to see different walls, within me, being torn down. A new level of personal healing and the rebuilding of my relationship with God began to take place. But, in the midst of all of this self-evaluation, self-determination, and rededication something happened. I found out I was seven weeks pregnant. Seven weeks pregnant, can you believe it?

I could believe it, but then again I couldn't. How did I let God down, again? How did I end up back in the similar situation 13 years later? Even though I asked these questions, I wasn't as disturbed as I was 13 years again.

This time, I was actually a mother. I knew what to expect when the baby arrives. My relationship with God is deeper, so what people said or how they felt didn't bother me. I wasn't living with my momma. I had a full-time job with benefits so when it's time to take my maternity leave I will still have income. I was a little more stable, so my adrenaline didn't rise too much, but what about school. I was finally pursuing a degree/career for me. I had finally put me first and here I was going to have to take time off to have a baby. What was I thinking?

Well, I'll tell you. I was thinking that I had got tired of living my life for others and being extra conscientious of the things that I was doing because I didn't want to offend anyone. Yes, I thought about how I was damaging my relationship with God, but I found myself justifying it by comparing myself to others and the things that I thought or actually knew they were doing.

Why did I have to always be the one to think about how my actions affected others? Were people thinking about how their actions were affecting me? My answer, "No."

I don't know what people were thinking. However, I do know that, at the time, I was being selfish and hurting so many people and wasn't thinking clearly. I wasn't intentionally trying to get pregnant, but during this time, my selfish thoughts were towards those that I had interactions with during my first pregnancy. I totally forgot about all the new relationships and people that God had since brought into my life.

During this season, I've learned, more than before, that no matter how things look in the physical realm, it's the spiritual realm that I must not take my eyes off. Meaning, many times we physically move on with our lives and as we're trying to rebuild, restructure, and redefine who we are, we tend to bring all our old baggage (i.e. guilt, hurt, pain, shame, blame, distrust, manipulation, complacency; just to name a few) into the new relationships without really realizing it. We think we're okay until something happens. For me, another pregnancy, and then we realize the mask that we've been unconsciously wearing.

It was easy for me to hide behind the hurt and distrust when I was sitting still. When I started moving, in my mind, I kept telling myself that those things didn't stop me, but made me stronger. Now, I wasn't lying to myself, but I wasn't being truthfully honest either. Those past endeavors didn't take me out, but they did have me build a wall for those to come that when I had to speak with members of my church as to why I could no longer participate in certain ministries, it tore me up inside. I cried before I told them, I cried after I told them, heck I probably just stopped crying, and I'm 8 months pregnant.

Adults, children, my son, my pastor, my church family was depending on me and in a selfish moment of forgetting who I was, I removed myself from the very table of the people that God allowed me to serve. You see my natural/physical family, as well as some of my church family, had been down this road with me before, but those that hadn't were the ones' that I've wept for and cried out to be forgiven for. They're the ones' that I had forgotten about. They're the ones' that I look at and pray, "Don't let my mishap be a stumbling block for them." Even in my indiscretions, I pray that I'm not the reason for another man's (male or female) down fall.

Looking in Elisha's eyes, once again, but this time he's 12 (almost 13) and seeing the hurt and disappointment that I've caused him, had me doubting every good thing that I had done. It had me thinking and asking, "Will I hurt this baby just the same?" When will I truly take me out of the picture and care about someone else. All these thoughts came into my mind, then a minister ministered to me and said, "God is removing all of the shame that the enemy has tried to bestow up on you." Then she said, "We all have iniquities. Mine can be in my heart. Yours just happened to show up as a baby."

The similar words that I used when I was being selfish are the words that God used, in love, to bring me out of my pit. I was advised to watch how I allowed this situation to affect me because Elisha was watching and whatever feelings I was carrying that he would carry them also. Although I believed every word, I didn't want to. Then again, how could I not?

Elisha has been through so much pain with me. The bond we share is so close that he can look in my eyes and tell when I'm upset or hurting. Never as a parent do you want your children to feel the need to carry your pain. But, I believe that when they've endured it with you from conception, you can't stop or change how they feel. All you can do is try to give them the best of what you've got left and pray that God carry them in the palm of His hands, just as He did you.

Writing this was a little difficult. When you've existed through your struggles and although you don't quite know how you made it, the fact that God didn't kill me in my sin and I'm still able to tell my story is a miracle. God knew my life story from the beginning until now, and even knows the ending. He knew that I was going to take a few pits stops along the way. His loving grace is that He knew I would give my children and my life, wholeheartedly, to Him.

My second son has not made his grand entrance yet, but God has already placed His hands upon him and declared that his name shall be Isaiah. Men of greatest and determination, to serve God and His people are the children that God has entrusted me with. As I continue to learn how to love my sons', through all of my pain, I know that I'll forever be a Student Mom.

LaMetria S. Johnson

Dear Student Moms,

    You deserve a reward just for the journey you are beginning. Balancing anything that requires your full attention with motherhood is rewarding in my book.

    I remember the rush I got walking out of the admissions office when I enrolled in school as a mom of four. This would not be my first time going to school with children; however, it did end up being the last. I appreciate meeting new people, and no matter what anyone says you learn a whole lot in those classes. Of course you won't apply every single thing you pick up to your day-to-day life, but you will walk away informed about every aspect and point of view of your career field.

    Only the strong survive, they say. Well, in my case that was the reason that I decided not to continue classes to obtain my degree. I began to think about how I was being buried in student loan debt for a piece of paper that I didn't need for anything that I decided I would do in the future. So just like that I dropped out.

    I have my days where I feel I should just complete the degree, which may take me less than a year to earn. I end up going back and forth in my mind because I don't like to waste time and money. Plus this debt has my credit looking ridiculous.

    Ultimately, you have to make decisions that compliment your life style and not ones that are based off of anyone's expectations of you. You are the only one that will pay your bills, and may be the only person at your commencement. That's how life goes and that's okay if it happens.

    I encourage any mother going to school to make sure that she's doing it for herself. Not for her children, not to follow in her mom's footsteps, and not because society expects you to go to college.

  I hope this reaches you and you understand that I am in no way trying to influence you to go or to not go to school. I want you to make a decision for yourself that will benefit your future.

Amber Farrar

3 THE FIRST TIME MOM

My first pregnancy seems to be the one that I remember every single detail about. When I found out that I was pregnant I wasn't in a stable living situation because my mother was very strict and I decided not to stay at her house. Ironically, she was the very first person I called when I knew what was going on. I cried to her and she said, "Come home." I lived at my mom's house for a few months at the beginning of my pregnancy, but for some reason, I just couldn't sit still.

I would go back and forth living at my grandma's house, but spending most nights with Dwaun, my three daughter's father. Dakai, Diya and Dumia were born years later. That went on until I was about eight months pregnant. I had gained so much weight that I couldn't get around anymore, and then I went back to my mom's house and became a complete couch potato.

I was an extremely spoiled little girl. My mom gave me a baby shower at her house. There were so many guests and gifts, and there was nowhere to sit. You know how it is when our people get together. There was not a chicken wing left for the pregnant girl. All four of my mom's brothers were at there and they bought everything big and expensive like always. I couldn't believe the love I got from all of our family and friends.

The night that I had signs of labor, I felt very sick. I vomited and believed something was about to happen. Amir is on his way. I told my mom and her exact words, "You would know if you were in labor. How are you going to act like a baby? And, you are about to have a baby."

Now the thought of what I experienced, makes me

laugh. However, at the moment, I felt horrible.

My favorite cousin that's more like a sister to me is Antwoinese. She stayed with me at my mom's house because I had complained about pain the week of delivery. She wanted to be with me in case Amir arrived any moment. So I thought. I lied in bed that night and cried and complained. Antwoinese and my mom ignored me. They said that I was so dramatic.

I woke up the following morning and that was it, I couldn't take any more pain. My mom called for Antwoinese to come on so we could head to the hospital, and this crazy girl had the nerve to say that she wasn't coming. I was about to go off on her. The entire ride from my mom's house to Barnes-Jewish Hospital, Antwoinese sang every R&B song that came on the radio. That was it. I had enough of her annoying sounds, and went off on her until I got to the labor and delivery room.

Fifteen years later, I can still hear Antwoinese singing the song, Love Calls by Kem.

My mom let everyone know that it was time and the family started to fill in the waiting room. My Aunt J came and turned into a doula. I suggest every mom has one. Aunt J helped me to calm down. Her love and support helped me make it through my labor with no epidural. However, I did receive some pain medicine through intravenous. But, I felt strong contractions and had emotional changes, both positive and negative, during labor and delivery.

I appreciate my mom and the rest of my family, wholeheartedly, for having my back from the very first time they heard of me being pregnant and still to this day. Even Dwaun was extra supportive. Although, he was disappointed because I told him that he had to wait until I came home from the hospital to see Amir.

Dwaun and I had been together almost every day since right after I found out that I was pregnant. He felt like he should be with me during labor and delivery because he would be with me after Amir and I were released from the hospital.

I didn't want a scene at the hospital. I knew that Amir's alleged dad would pop up. And, sure as shit stinks, he did with a few of his friends. He said, "So you did what you wanted and just had a baby anyway." If I had not just delivered a baby, I would have given him a pumpkin head.

Amir Shakur was my mom's first grandchild and my grandma's first great-grandchild. He and I being spoiled was an understatement. Amir wasn't just my baby. He belonged to my entire family. Our entire village truly helped raise him in the first years of his life.

I was young and couldn't sit still even after the birth of Amir. I loved him with all of my heart, but I liked to hang out with my friends and I continued to do that while being a new mom. Most of my friends were having their first babies too. You'd think that would make us all want to start a moms club or something, but that's the opposite of what happened.

During Amir's early months, he and I stayed with my mom and brothers. Soon as I was about to leave the house, my mom would ask, "What time will you be back?" She believed even though Amir was a baby, he should wake up and see me. Sometimes I would not return home at the time we discussed, and she would call to ask, "Where are you?" Then before I could reply, she would say, "You should be at home. Come get your baby." This happened nearly every time I left the house.

Amir was about seven months when Dwaun and I had

moved into our first apartment together. It wasn't far from where Seth, my biological dad, lived. Amir and I visited him and his family regularly at first.

During this time, I thought Seth and I were establishing a relationship, and his family and I were becoming pretty close. His youngest daughter helped with Amir all of the time. She loved to do it, and I needed her to care for him.

It was out of the question to take him to my mom's or my grandma's house without having to argue with my mom about me leaving Amir with everybody. She thought I should be with him 24-7 because I didn't work.

Shortly after Dwaun and I moved in together, he went to the county jail for 10 of the longest months ever. That slowed me down completely. I didn't have my boyfriend to run out of town with or be wherever else with all day.

I've always been protective of my baby boy. Even though Dwaun's family accepted Amir as one of their own, I wanted to keep him out of their way and around his real blood. Amir was with Seth's daughter or at my grandma's house with her or our cousins.

I remember Dwaun's mom asking, "What's your problem? Why are you with a man and don't let him claim your baby?"

Dwaun and I had been together every single day. As much as I tried, there was no convincing her of the truth, which was that Amir did not belong to her son at all.

To this day, everyone that thinks they know Dwaun and me believe that Amir is his biological son. I never went around saying that and neither did Dwaun. He used to tell Amir that he was his rental pop.

Dwaun was an audition away from being a comedian. He was always saying something silly like that. He and I both wanted Amir to understand the truth about our situation.

My Uncle Anthony introduced Amir to sports at age four, and transported him daily to and from a practice or a game. Amir was with him at sport events just about all of the time. He would come home right before it got late, like he was age 12. The boy was much younger.

Our Uncle Anthony became heavily involved with Amir's after school and weekend activities. Now, Amir was age five. I had two more children, Dakai and Diya, and was pregnant with Dumia. And, Dwaun had passed away.

After that, my children and I were back at my grandma's house around the clock. We were around my family a lot, more than ever before.

More people than I know have loved Amir. Everyone thought that he was my uncle's son. People who saw them together regularly had no idea that I was Amir's mom.

Now, I had Amir and the girls. My uncle's help with Amir would come in handy.

I got tired of not being able to support all four of my kids, I couldn't be everywhere all the time. So, when Amir was age 10, I became a cheer coach for his football team and guess who my first cheerleaders were? Yes, my daughters, The Valley Girls. In my mind, it was one of the best decisions I had made as a mom.

I ended up coaching the team for three years and the experiences were sweet. I got to run down the sideline with Amir, my firstborn, while he scored touchdowns and threw game-winning passes. I loved it!

At the age of thirty-four, I think back to what occurred

with me as an 18-year-old mom. And, how I wouldn't do half the things I did before ever again. I wouldn't repeat some of the same things that I did with my second, third or fourth child either.

I had my fourth child ten plus years ago. In no way am I being hard on myself, but there's no way a 34-year-old woman and an 18-year-old girl should think alike anyway. I do not regret a thing.

My life has made me strong, fearless, and full of faith. I have learned from many mistakes and I have figured out that what work for others may not work for me. The same vice versa. And, that's okay.

You have to get comfortable with doing things your way with knowing how to balance being able to accept advice. Growing is beautiful, and so is learning and experiencing new and different things.

When Amir first entered the world, I received some support from his biological father. I believed that if we dated, he would have no problem being a friend and helping me to take care of our child. Since that hasn't happened, he hasn't displayed that he wants to be active in Amir's life. I don't bother him at all and Amir has no desire to either.

I think the year was 2014 when Amir's dad contacted him. I was surprised and happy. At the time, I was living by myself in downtown St. Louis with just my four children. I remember saying to him that if he had any plans on speaking to Amir and then going missing, to forget about connecting. He agreed that he wouldn't.

I allowed him to come see Amir at my grandma's house. She was so excited to see this fool. It was crazy. My grandma saw something in him that I couldn't see.

He was good to me when we were dating, but he was a completely different person when we had to parent together. He showed up for a couple of weeks throwing money around and just like that he disappeared.

I didn't see or hear from him until about two years later. I think I offended him by telling him he needs to support Amir financially. Our conversation went from how he missed us and he was sorry to oh my wife said, "You would talk about financial responsibility first." I never understand this guy because we were never in a relationship and I thought we had an understanding that we were friends.

Well, friends don't leave each other hanging and that's what he did. Nevertheless, I took care of my baby with support from my family and my daughter's dad. I never pressed any child support issue or tried finding him and giving him a shakedown either. It was what it was.

Sometimes I forget that he exists, no lie. I could never have respected this man the way that he wanted me to anyway. My uncles raised me to make sure that any man in my life could protect and provide for me. This person could only handle one of those things, so I thought it was best for us to be friends and he was lucky for that.

I protected my friends, male and female, so I expected the same at that time in my life.

When I found out that I was pregnant with Amir, the alleged dad asked, "Are you pregnant with my child?" I said, "No." Obviously, I didn't believe I was pregnant with his child. I hadn't considered myself in love with him, and barely had interaction with him. How could I be pregnant with his child? Plus, I dated someone else, who cared deeply for my unborn child and me. Although, I cheated on my boyfriend, he had promised to protect me from the alleged dad, but hurt us both if we wanted to debate about Amir's paternity.

Amir's dad knew this and said nothing. So neither did I and that's the story on how Amir has a name that doesn't belong to his father nor me.

My boyfriend at the time was a real hot boy and a jerk. He was physical with me one time too many. He knew that I was pregnant, and would still be rough or abusive.

I broke up with him when I was two months pregnant. I met Dwaun when I was three months pregnant. I'm glad we met him because I had no desire to reach out to my old boyfriend or anyone else after that.

Once in 2016, I received a letter in the mail from Family Support stating that Amir would lose his Medicaid if I didn't complete a child support application. I contacted his father to inform him about what was happening. Instead of coming up with a solution, this guy says, "My wife said that you just want to put me on child support." I was furious. I don't know his wife and she doesn't know anything about me for a fact.

I never really acknowledged this man as Amir's dad. I thought I was helping him. Absent fathers love to complain about court systems catching up with them, so I was nice enough to give him a heads up. I don't know how neither he nor she could have made himself or herself believe what they were saying. I felt completely insulted. A bit confused also.

A paternity test had been done through the state. I hadn't done anything else.

Anyway, I don't care what the alleged father felt. I just wanted him to know what was going on. But, you better believe that after the conversation, I wanted his head on a platter. I felt he owed me half for every pair of socks, t-shirts, and underwear.

I thank God for timing. My husband talked me out of giving the situation any more energy. I was over it all, in an instant.

Maybe twice in Amir's 15 years on earth, I asked him if he would like to contact his dad. He answered, "No."

Since Amir was about a 1-year-old baby, I've never received support from his dad financially. I have no ill feelings towards him and I wish him the best in life. I know that I'm not responsible for what Amir's dad does as a parent or a person period. He has a higher power to answer to than Amir or me.

I hope one day, he realizes that and contacts his child, and does right by the other people in his life. Amir has many siblings from his dad. He talks to a couple of his brothers. They were introduced to each other through sports. I think that's pretty cool.

I encourage Amir to be an awesome son, brother, family member, friend and citizen. When he's in contact with anyone related to him or a friend of our family it is always nothing but love out the gate.

The relationship that I have with Amir is very special and different from my other children. I feel like Amir is my first love. We have experienced so much together. He had more time and memories to enjoy with the girl's dad than they did. By him being the oldest, a lot of the decisions that I have made for my family, I considered Amir first.

The relationship with Amir has taught me so much about becoming a mother and growing without beating myself up about mistakes. There's no manual to motherhood. Being the best you can be with love will take you a long way.

Amber Farrar

4 THE TEEN MOM

We're all born to die. That's a fact. Everything else about our lives is statistic based. How we choose to live out our days all depends on our individual selves. Each and every one of us has a path created and designed just for us. No matter how hard you might think you know best, remember God is the creator of all things. He knows what we want and all that we need. Our responsibility is to trust Him and His word.

I believe strongly that nothing happens by chance. Any and everything that happens throughout our days happens as a testament of God's will. Sometimes we have to be very careful of what we ask for because you might get exactly that, nothing more and nothing less.

Take me for example, I was your typical teenage girl, at least I thought so. All I wanted to do, as a teenager, was to hang out with my friends and do stupid teenage stuff. The only thing that ever rained on my parade, was going to my father's house.

As a kid, I loved every second of the visits to my father's house. He spoiled my little sister and me rotten. We were the youngest two of his many children. I was about to turn age 13, and no longer wanted really to hang out with my dad and younger sister every weekend and school vacation.

I wanted to laugh and joke, and occasionally say curse words. You know, live on the edge a little.

My father didn't play. If he ever came to pick me up and I wasn't there or prepared to go once he got there, meaning if he had to look for me, there was going to be problems. Although, he'd never disciplined me physically. His words were enough. He had one of the deepest voices I'd ever heard. I hated to hear him fuss. So, I tried very hard to always be obedient.

I wasn't perfect. But, in the eyes of both my parents, I was unflawed. They always made me believe that I was too. My mom talked my father into letting me stay home a few weeks that summer. I wanted to make a little pocket change and her friend let me work at her beauty shop. My father agreed to the experience. He was an old-fashioned southerner that believed in children earning their keep.

I was relieved. My father didn't live in the neighborhood. Whenever I left the hood, so much was missed.

I had so many friends. We were all very tight like sisters, and still are to this day. I was the youngest of the crew, but just as advanced as they were in age. I could talk any talk and walk any walk. All you had to do was try me, and you'd see that I wasn't the one to play with.

One time I was away, everyone in the crew got booed up. I didn't get the memo. I liked boys, but they weren't really into me. I was a Tomboy. I played sports, and beat up boys. No boy was going to like me that way. I ended up being the wingman. I was like their matchmaker.

It wasn't until I saw this one boy that made me rethink everything I'd ever thought about my relationship with boys. He was so fine! He had the prettiest big brown eyes and his skin was the perfect caramel complexion.

I couldn't even talk around him because he was so damn fine! He lived across the alley and everyone knew him. I couldn't understand how I'd never seen him before.

I went to Pint, one of my friends, and told her how I felt about him and with no hesitation she told me, "NO." She explained to me that he wasn't the type of boy I needed to talk to, and I asked, "Why not?" She went on to tell me that he'd already talked to several other girls in the neighborhood, including her sister. I guess he thought he was Tupac because the brother was getting around. I let it go, for that moment.

I started talking to a guy who was much older than me. He and I were just alike, awkwardly weird. I lied to him about my age. I told him that my age was 14, totally skipped my true age 13. He was age 15, about to be a sophomore in high school.

I started to feel like I was finally on the same page as everyone else now that I had a friend. He was the totally opposite of what's his name, but he was fine too.

We talked all the time, and discovered that both of us came from blended families. We got along very well. I'm pretty sure he thought about sex, but it wasn't a thing.

After summer was over, my family and I ended up moving on the next block over and one house away from you know whom. Now with only one house separating us, I hated the sight of him. And, once I'd gotten to know a little bit about him, I realized that I couldn't stand him.

He was probably the most conceded person I'd ever met. From what I knew of him, he stayed with his grandma because his mom died when he was eight years old and everyone loved him. He hung out with the older guys in the neighborhood, but wasn't that much older than me.

The following summer, the Avenue was popping. Barbecues and house parties were the new normal. While sitting on my porch, up walks what's his name, Mr. Pretty eyes, at least that's what I called him in my head. He started talking to my friend and telling how mean I was to him. He started going on and on about how he knew I liked him and was just scared of him.

He was so right. I replied by saying that I wasn't scared and I could show him better than I could tell him.

Now, I have no idea where that attitude came from because I had never done much at all beyond kissing. But, on that day and a month away from my 14th birthday, I lost my virginity in the most unconventional way. Trying to prove a point.

I allowed him to have something that I could never get back. And, I knew it the moment I saw him. I never took heave to the information that was told to me about him when we first met. I fell in lust.

Behind my parents back, I had sex every chance I got. A few months later I told him that I'd missed my period and I didn't know what to do.

He convinced me that we were going to have our baby. Like a dummy, I agreed to keep my child if in fact I was pregnant.

My mom must have felt that something wasn't right because on a routine doctor's visit, she had them to give me a pregnancy test. Her even having the thought in her mind flabbergasted me. I thought I'd never given her any indication that I was sexually active, but she was dead on.

I tried to buy myself time by putting water in my sample, hoping it would throw off the results. That didn't work. When the doctor came back into the room to read the results, I saw the disappointment in my mother's eyes. The doctor confirmed that I was pregnant.

My mother immediately contacted my father to deliver the news to him. Without any hesitation, he told her, "It's your fault!" After I listened to them go back and forth about wherever they went wrong as parents, which was something they had badly, I felt like shit!

The next eight months changed my life in more ways than one. I tried to keep the pregnancy a secret at first because I had no idea what my parents were going to make me do.

I'd returned home from a visit to my dad's house and found out that my new baby daddy actually had two kids on the way. He'd been with someone I'd consider to be my friend. She wasn't like one of my sisters, but I brought her into our circle.

Of course, my new baby daddy lied to me and said that she was lying. He told me that nobody wanted to see us together, and I believed him.

The art of manipulation is to gain someone's trust and distort the truth with lies. His handle worked until I went to see her myself. On that day, I realized someone could look you right in your eyes and lie to your face with no hesitation.

I don't know if he was hoping or actually praying for the baby not to be his child, but he knew it was. At first sight, without a blood test, I knew that was definitely his baby boy. The baby looked just like his father had pushed him out of his own body during labor and delivery. I couldn't believe that the father would lie and deny his own flesh and blood like that, but he did.

I went home with a piece of my heart broken that night. A little too late, I started to understand why I should've stayed away from him in the first place. Needless to say, there was neither excitement nor congratulations for me.

I guess a lot of people couldn't find joy during my pregnancy. In their eyes, I was still a child myself.

I could've had an abortion and hid my indiscretions like most of the people that sat high and looked low on me, but my parents decided that I needed to learn my lesson. Honestly I was more afraid to get the abortion than to give birth.

In today's world things are much different. Abortions are pretty much another form of birth control basically. Even the ways people celebrate babies are different now. I've seen some creative gender reveals, baby showers and maternity shoots. I could only dream of moments like that during my pregnancy.

The news of someone expecting is so bittersweet for me. I think it's because of the way I was welcomed into motherhood. As a matter of fact, I wasn't welcomed at all.

What I got was a lot of conversations about me that never actually included me. I felt judged and alone from the start.

One of my favorite people in the world even went so far as comparing me to a crack head. Telling me that my child, the baby girl that I was carrying and could feel her heart beating through my body, wouldn't be anything because I wouldn't be shit. She told me that I wouldn't be able to take care of my baby girl and she would end up being a snotty nose, pissy baby.

I can laugh at it now because those words really made me go hard. So now, I thank her. She pushed me. I'd just wished we could've used that moment to get closer. Instead, it pushed me away from her.

My family delayed a moment of growth focusing on the wrong thing. My mother and big sister at that time, were the only two people that told me I would be okay. They loved me in a way that still poured hope into my life. That's what I needed most of all.

I knew I wasn't a bad person. Also, I also knew that I'd made some bad decisions and they led me to some unfortunate situations. But, I never doubted for a second that I could or would make something out of myself.

I talked to my baby girl every day and although she

couldn't talk back, I knew she heard me. If anyone in the world understood me, it would be my child while still in my womb. She let me know it too. Before making it into this world we were connected like Method Man and Mary. She was all I needed to get by.

During my pregnancy, I was severely anemic and my blood pressure was extremely high. I'd had enough of what everyone else had to say about my life and me. I needed to come up with my own plan if I was going to prove them all wrong.

I was diagnosed with preeclampsia and was admitted into the hospital. I stayed there until they decided to induce labor. After almost a week in the hospital, on Sunday, August 31, 1997 at six o'clock a.m. the nurses entered my room to induce labor.

Without a soul in sight, the time had finally come to meet Cynthia. The day that I found out my baby was a girl, I decided to name her after my grandmother, who she'd never meet, but be connected always to her.

In my mind, I thought labor and delivery would be like the experience in the movies. I would scream and shout, and then push and voila' she'd make an appearance. It went totally a different way.

I ended up falling to sleep for a few hours, and woke up to the news about the tragic death of Princess Diana. The nurse that was prepping the room for my delivery leaned over and told me not to worry about that because in a few minutes I would give the world another princess.

As the contractions started to overtake me, the nurse to me that I couldn't get an epidural because I was dilated seven centimeters. So, I started to push momentarily. My heart instantly began to race. At that moment, all I wanted was my momma.

As the tears started to fall from my face, the nurse told me to wrap my arms around her and to push when the doctor instructed me to do so. I pushed, and then I rested each time the pain got more intense. After an hour of active labor at 12:37 p.m., I gave birth to a 6lb 7oz beautiful baby girl. I named her Cynthia Danielle Nicole Oliphant. She was perfect from head to toe. I had received the perfect A after failing so many tests.

There was no turning back now. At the tender age of 15, I became a mother. I instantly called everyone I knew. My mother was the very first person. "She's here," I said full of joy.

Every Labor Day weekend, my family had a picnic. My entire family came to see my baby girl soon as they learned she'd arrived. For the first time, in what seemed like forever, I was happy.

I was discharged on what should've been my first day of high school. My big sister came to take me from the hospital to home. During our time together, she assured me that I was going to be fine.

My mom's insurance paid for me to have a tutor for the six weeks that I would be home, so that I didn't get behind in my schoolwork. She only came three times a week, but I would do all the assignments at once making her constantly have to get more. By the time I went back to school, I had already passed all my classes for the semester, which allowed me to finish the school year with extra credits and more freedom in school years ahead. That was my plan. But, I definitely didn't want to draw any extra attention to myself. I was already known at school as the "girl with the baby."

I tried my best to hang in there with school. I knew

that finishing school would make my parents proud, but I was living a very complicated life. Sometimes, the issues at school became secondary to what was going on at home.

Not really sure on how to handle the pressure of being a teenage parent, I tried to find solitude in my child's father. But, I learned that he was fighting his own battles.

As if keeping up with world history and physics wasn't hard enough. I had to hide busted lips and black eyes from everyone so I started missing school. I barely made it through sophomore year because my grades were dropping from being absent. Not to mention, I couldn't stop getting into trouble. I got suspended for smoking weed on the school bus, and they wanted me out.

Part of the consequences for my actions was to attend an alternative school. I was placed in a program to earn my way back to school.

My parents were great providers, but they weren't very involved in much else concerning me because they could never see eye to eye, which made it easier to lie to them.

I went to the alternative school for a while, until I clashed with one of the teachers. I didn't like to be singled out.

When people think they know your story, they automatically think they have you pegged out.

The teacher treated me horribly and I wasn't having it. All I had to do was my work, and I'd be able to return back to my home school. That never happened. The teacher told me if I didn't like how she taught her class, I could leave it and I did. She put me out and not even knowing how to get back to St. Louis Avenue, I hopped on the first bus I saw.

I wanted to work anyway, so I could make my own

money and have full control of my life. I thought it was the only way. I got my first job at McDonald's, and worked the morning shift when I was supposed to be in class.

Neither one of my parents knew I had dropped out of school. When they finally found out, they both explained to me what it is like being grown. And since I wanted to be grown, then grown is what I would have to be.

I mostly stayed with my mom from that point on. She started gambling shortly after that so between her long work hours and her new aggressive habit, I never really saw her. I spent most of my time with my child's father, with no supervision because I was now grown.

I continued to have unprotected sex, and ended up pregnant once again. Now, I was definitely raised better than what I displayed.

I started to feel so ashamed of myself because if I didn't break their hearts with Cynthia, finding out that I got myself right back in the same situation would do it for sure. So this time, I deeply considered having an abortion. I wasn't in the position to take care of another child. Even though, I was handling my situation well.

This time was different from the last pregnancy. I kept this to myself.

I made an appointment at Planned Parenthood. During the consultation, I was made aware of exactly how far along the pregnancy was and the amount of the procedure.

I worked hard to save the money to take care of my problem, but was told that because I was further alone it would be more than what I thought it would be. After charging me for an ultrasound and a pregnancy test, I was released with one of the biggest burdens I ever could've put on myself.

Some days, I would come in the house and my mom would be in tears. It broke my heart to see her so upset.

That wasn't my first time seeing her cry, but it was different from the other times. I thought, maybe she was missing my brothers. Now that both my brothers were gone and I was never at home and she was all alone.

Part of me couldn't help but think maybe she blamed herself for me not reaching the expectations she had for me. I couldn't really tell because she'd started being cold towards me and we were no longer as close as we once were.

About a week later, I came home and she told me that we were getting put out. She gave me two options either move with my father or go with her back to my grandmother's house. I didn't understand how we had gotten here because she made good money, but gambling had started to overpower her life. I knew that neither one of those places was where I wanted live. I called my brother and he sent me a bus tickets to Springfield, Mo.

That bus ride was full of emotions. I cried the entire time just thinking about how much my life had changed so fast. I could never go back. I didn't want to face the reality that I'd messed up my life, and that maybe every person that spoke about me was speaking the truth.

The night I arrived in Springfield, bags still in my brother's trunk, the police kicked in the door. No one was arrested because they didn't find whatever they were looking for.

Lost in everything that was going on, I wondered how I was going to make it to better days. I started frequently going into the bathroom and just crying.

Most nights, I cried out to God for help. Hadn't

realized that I was in fact praying. At that time, I didn't know how to ask for forgiveness. And, the more I cried out the worst I felt.

I owned everything I'd done that got me to the point I was at. That type of accountability was good, but I was still barely surviving. Everyone knew of my wrongs, but nobody else wanted to take accountability for their part in my whirlwind of issues.

My mother was no longer available to be that force I needed to remain sane. She was dealing with her own battles in life. I just kept it all in. Still pregnant, the situation was way worse than before because I had absolutely nobody. My brothers did all they could for me, but they were young too, only age 19 and 20 themselves.

I found a job at the mall and out of nowhere I started showing. My brothers were surprised, and I acted like I was too. I had to be about four or five months pregnant by now. My brothers never judged or criticized me. They gave me that same unconditional love my mom gave so I surrounded myself around them.

I'd gotten baptized while I was pregnant with Cynthia, but it wasn't until now that I'd started following some of the things I'd been taught. I started to pray more often because it gave me hope. I couldn't give up failure was never an option. One thing I knew for sure at my young age was God would never leave nor forsake me.

I found an OBGYN close by, and started getting prenatal care so my baby would be healthy. Something I'd learned while being pregnant with Cynthia was that no matter how much, talking to someone seemed like it helped. But, keeping it to myself just made more sense.

I learned to adapt to my new surroundings and it kept me grounded for a while. My brother provided room and board so I was able to save money. I even enrolled back in school.

Some days I still desperately cried myself to sleep. I missed everyone, but convinced myself I was in a better place.

I didn't fit in anywhere. There's a reality show now about being sixteen and pregnant, but in 1998 I lived it in my everyday life. For me, when things started to seem better they often actually got worst.

My health had become an issue at the end of my first pregnancy, but evolved much faster with the second. It seemed that I was producing more cancer cells than normal, which was said to be common for pregnant women. I was tested for cervical cancer and because I was in a smaller city, I needed to go back to St. Louis to get further tested. Dreading any more bad news I declined going to see another doctor for a second opinion. I made sure I took care of myself the best I knew how. I continued to work until my final month, and every day was a struggle.

My mom talked me into to coming back home to make sure I was okay, and I instantly got a bus ticket. I really wanted to be there. I did not want to go through labor and delivery alone. I'd already experienced that and I really needed at least my momma.

My mom along with one of my friends picked me up from the bus station about 11' o clock p.m. on March 2, 1999. I instantly felt better just being home. When we pulled up to my grandma's house, it was just like it was when I left. House filled with my family full of high energy. My oldest cousin was also there playing Yahtzee with my grandma. Man I really missed everybody. Tired of watching them I went over on the Avenue to be around my friends.

It's like as soon as I sat down and relaxed I had to get up. I had this pressure on my back that wasn't letting up. Pint asked me was I ok and I told her that I was fine, but I honestly didn't know what was going on. It was starting to scare me because I knew why I'd come back home. As I tried to walk back to my grandma house, the pressure had gotten so intense I couldn't walk at all. I was in labor. Pint drove me back to my grandma house. An ambulance arrived and my cousin road with me to the hospital. This was all knew to me, my first labor went smoothly. This one was going a totally different way.

I felt every contraction, which made me want the epidural as soon as I could get it. Because I just ate, I kept throwing up. It was horrible. I was surprised, but relieved that my cousin was there the entire time. She made sure I was okay from the beginning to the end. Besides teaching me the Lord's Prayer as a kid, we really didn't have any memories together.

On March 3, 1999 at 1:04 a.m. my cousin became a major part of my life. She helped me welcome another healthy baby girl 7lbs 4oz. Tonasia Mornea Oliphant was here and ready for the world.

My mom wanted me to name Cynthia Asia, but instead I named her after her father's mother. So my cousin, who had named me, and I conjoined the letters ton and asia and came up with Tonasia.

Thankfully my cancer scare was just that, everything was okay.

After released from the hospital, I stayed with my dad at his house. Things were not the same there at all. My stepmom had passed away the year before. It was because of her that my dad was so supportive after Cynthia was born.

Something that hadn't changed at my dad's house was my little sister being there. As always, every weekend she came over. She was actually very helpful. It kind of broke my heart that I wasn't a better role model for her. I constantly told her to do better and to use my life as a learning tool to teach her what not to do. I wasn't there long because I was ready to go back home. I'd planned on going back to Springfield six weeks after I gave birth.

While I was in St. Louis, my children's father had found a place in Springfield. So, I decided to move out of my brothers' apartment and in with him.

My dad showed love, the way he knew how. He got me furniture, an Italian leather bone white living room set and a bed. It was only a studio apartment we didn't need much. My dad paid my uncle to drive it back in a U-Haul truck. I guess you can say no matter how much I thought I messed up, he still spoiled me.

I said my goodbyes, and went to my new house. We made it there early in the morning. My uncle told me he'd come unload the truck later that day.

Totally waiting to meet his new baby, my children's dad came and helped us into the house. I couldn't really get the feel of the apartment because it was so late. I just wanted to go to sleep. He woke me up and asked me if my brother was to pick the kids and me up or if he needed to drop us off.

I knew exactly what he was implying. Although it hurt to hear, I simply answered, without shedding a tear, "I'll have him to pick us up." I couldn't believe that nigga. He talked a million dollars' worth of shit and when it was time to step up he didn't. I was disappointed, but not defeated.

When I left that morning, it would be a year before I talked to him again. We lived in the same city and it seemed like we were strangers. The dynamic that I thought my children would have was no longer a part of my thoughts. I wanted a family, but it looked like I was going to be a single mother.

I turned seventeen that summer and I was tired of living in secret so I went home to St. Louis. I had to get use to the way life was now. My mom was at my grandma's house and my dad was still set in his ways, but his doors were always open to me. So I moved back with him, but stayed with friends often. I wasn't allowed to come in his house after 11:00 p.m. Anyways so if it was late, I pretty much didn't bother going home.

My cousin, who I'd named Tonasia after, let me stay at her house sometime. That was way easier for me to maneuver on my own. The metro link was across from her apartment.

I enrolled St. Louis Job Corps Center so that I could finally finish school. I got a job at Famous and Barr through the retail sales program.

My life had been a shit show for two straight years. One bad thing happened after another. I lost all aspirations for myself. If I didn't know how to do anything, I knew how to roll my sleeves up and try to fix whatever I thought I'd broken. But, I was what was broken.

With two kids, I never thought about myself. They were always my first priority.

I received my high school diploma at St. Louis Job Corps Center in October 1999. I was proud of myself. I did it! I finished school for Cynthia and Tonasia.

The best thing that I could've ever done for my children and myself was to strengthen my relationship with God. I believed that if I dedicated myself to the Lord, my children and their lives would be blessed.

Over the next seven years, I had three more children Reggie, Amorion, and Jabori. I still had struggles. I dragged my five children along and endured countless of life altering, meaningless changes and situations, which more than likely affected their thoughts about how life should be. I sacrificed everything for my children because they're all blessings God gave me.

Whatever you do in life make sure you seek and find your purpose. Then give it a hundred percent, no matter how many people try to deter you away from your destiny. Stick to your purpose during life's distractions. Don't give up.

At the age of fifteen, yes, I was told that I would not make it and would never be shit because I got pregnant. That stuck with me. For years, I let the statement beat me up. Now, I thank God for my life every day. Some days I'll admit, a thank you prayer isn't the very first thing I do when I get up, but each and every day I do thank him for continuously giving me chance after chance to make things better than the days before.

Becoming a teenage mother was hard and it definitely had its up and downs. I went through things, physically, mentally and emotionally, that were unexplainable to someone that had not reached that level of understanding. I often felt alone because most adults treated me like teenage motherhood was a punishment and a shame, instead of supporting me and teaching me how to embrace it. And for that reason, I hated myself and I hated my life. It seemed like I was forced to live this life. I had no positivity being spoken unto me.

With great maturity and understanding, I realized that I chose my life and that I was never alone. The village that raised me, helped me raised my children. And, I had to speak good over myself. This is a message that my big sister, who also was a teenage mom, helped me realize and always told me it every time we spoke. Also, realized my life was a gift not only for me, but for my children and for anyone's life I could help with my testimony.

Life should be a learning experience for both the parent as well as the child. As parents, we shouldn't think we have all the answers because that's not always the case. Remember that we were adolescence who made mistakes. Honestly, think about how we've learned important life lessons. Might not be some of your proudest moments, but because you made it through that ordeal, you can testify to others that it, too, shall surely pass.

If you apply that affirmation to your children, with the necessary commentary, it will help them develop a mindset of positivity and success. You'll be surprised at the level of communication and connection between you and them.

That's what saves families, communicating and earning together how to execute the problem so it has no room to grow any bigger than it needs to be. In doing, you'll learn your child and your child will learn you.

God sends us our children. He helps us to grow, to fertilize them at whatever age.

It's like we've forgot how to care with our whole hearts. I've always loved with my full heart and because at that I've allowed myself to accept less. It caused heartache and pain that I wasn't deserving of.

One of life's greatest discernment's is to exegete what

you've been through in order to grow from it. I had to redefine and replace, give new definition to the pains that had started to define me. We often spend a lifetime living in our sorrows and our regrets, and fearful of places, people and the powers to heal.

Ultimately, if the truth isn't found in God then we've wasted a life in an abyss over spiritualization. Let me explain. I ask for most of what I experienced, the other part wasn't for me it was for the people I encountered during my life including both my parents. God's plan for me was out my hands and when I finally realized that and gave him full control, He took me somewhere I never could've imagined being.

I thought that I was taking one loss after another, doing something wrong. The reality, I wasn't losing, I was gaining.

Throughout my life, I've gained strength, faith, peace, mercy, grace, love and happiness. If you don't stand in your truth, you will not move forward.

I say what I should've done because I've grown from everything in life, including being a teenage mother. Faith taught me that worrying would enjoy your life for you if you give it the power to do so.

Get to know your flaws. We have to learn to acknowledge to our bad behaviors and weaknesses and attend to them. An inspirational speaker spoke on it best. We can create a new reality for ourselves within seventeen seconds.

It's been over 22 years, and I've spent a lot of time proving points. Now, I do what's asked of me, and watch God work. I've owned Infinite Solutions LLC, my own marketing and consulting business, since fall 2015. I work with over a dozen black owned businesses throughout the metropolitan area.

I've watched front and center as three of my children earned their high school diplomas. My oldest struggled to keep her head focused, but finished a year ahead of her class and my second eldest finished Summa Cum Laude. Every achievement of my children, I stand with them proudly because I know they were born to be great.

Ask God for what you want and believe He will give you your whatever. Trust Him. It will be yours. You'll have to put it the work, but little victories lead to great successes.

Jamina Beal

I wouldn't consider myself as "fass" as the old folks use to say. I was a little girl that just so happen to have a boyfriend. I met him at a party when I was 12-years-old, one month before my 13th birthday. We exchanged numbers and talked on the phone every single day. I was 14-years-old when we finally saw each other in person again. By this time I was not sure about him but I thought I was in love, and had already planned my life out with him. Not because I was "fass", but because I thought I knew what I wanted. At 14, I was already writing our names down on paper as a family. Carlos, Nicole, Carlos Jr., and Carlisha Coleman. Yeah I was 14-years-old, and thought I had everything figured out.

I knew better, but I did it anyway. He did say that he loved me. We hung out all of the time. He bought me stuff. He was my man, so why not have sex with him? We'd even said that we were going to get married when we got older. Plus we had been talking since I was 12-years-old and I'm now 15-years-old, and scared as shit because I'm pregnant.

I broke the news to my parents. I knew they would be disappointed and they were. We decided (well our parents decided) that abortion was right for us at that time, with us being so young.

Procedure day was the scariest day of my life! I'm a 15-year-old child lying on a bed having a life taken from me. I can remember lying there and wondering if my unborn child was a boy or girl. Would I ever be able to have kids again? I was severely upset with my parents for making me abort my child, August 1992.

October 1992, I was pregnant again! I was ashamed. I went to school and work basically hiding from my parents. I knew for sure that this time, they would KILL me!

I called myself showing them (whenever they found out) that I was ready to be a parent. I was saving my work checks, and my baby daddy's money that he gave me to provide for our child. I went to the clinic and signed up for free medical insurance and prenatal care. I was on it! I knew I could do it. I didn't want to get another abortion.

My parents found out that I was pregnant at seven months. Again disappointed and probably disgusted at me to say the least. My dad said that since I wanted to be grown, I had to be grown and move out. I packed my things, called my baby's daddy, and left.

I stayed with my him and his family for about two weeks before my momma called and made me come home. But, by this time, I had set a goal.

My plan was to get an apartment of my own by the time our baby was born. I had no idea that you needed first and last month rent, along with a security deposit in order to move in an apartment. But, I had a goal and that is what mattered most.

Our baby was born July 1993. I can remember like yesterday, lying in that hospital bed scared as shit! Thinking what am I going to do with a baby, a whole human that belongs to me?

My baby's daddy and I sat in the hospital nursery feeding our son. We were just kids ourselves and all of the nurses and other parents in the nursery stared at us. They made me feel like we were incapable of being parents just like them. That's a moment I will never forget. I knew I'd never see those people again, but I was determined to prove them and every other person who'd tried to shame us wrong.

So, I always call my son my push child! Because of

him I am who I am today. I want to make sure that we beat the odds.

We've been through a lot, but we've persevered. My baby's daddy and I have been husband and wife for 18 years, May 2020. We now have a 13-year-old daughter.

Our son, who was born to teen parents, is doing great! He graduated from high school and moved to a new state, and has a good job and is engaged to be married. We beat the odds.

Nicole Tucker-Coleman

Dear Teen Mom,

      Listen, I want to encourage you. I know how you feel. I've been right there. You will experience emotional and life changes. Know that it is all right.

      Everybody will want to give you advice on what you should, shouldn't and should've done. All of that is great! But, it's about you and your baby now.

      Keep your head clear. Be open-minded. And, stay stress free! Set goals for you and your baby. The sky is the limit. I'm rooting for you.

Love,
Nicole Tucker-Coleman, Teen Mom 1993

5 THE STAY AT HOME MOM

First off, I would like to apologize for thinking of being a stay at home mom as vacationing, living off your husband's money and relaxing all day. I didn't realize all the expectations of being a nurturing mother nor imagine me feeling up and down and taking a huge risk of a full-time mom. What was I thinking? This was not for me.

I was a working, independent woman with goals and dreams, which were put on hold so that my husband would lead the way. Be head of the household and take care of his family.

Yes, of course that is what he told me so I took his word for it. Was I making a mistake? Is he setting me up? Will he leave me after a while? What do I expect from this knowing damn well I said I would never be a stay at home mom?

In 2016, I got pregnant with my third child. My husband and I started planning for the future and looking at our finances, work schedules, and babysitters. Of course, one of the things had to go. Financially, it did not add up for what we had planned. At the moment, I knew I had to give up my job. I'd worked there for nine years to give my kids everything that they deserved.

There were pros and cons to both parents working full-time. There is the cost of raising and supporting a family, and having two incomes and no time. Yet completely, both parents are responsible for balancing work and sharing parenting and household. How are we going to balance our work life and our family lives? If we continued with our careers, who was going to be our children safe base?

Me, of course, I was not expecting no one to support our family needs continuously for the sake of both parents work life. So we had to do what was best for the Easley's. We decided I had to raise our children.

An angel, Kobi Easley, was born at Missouri Baptist. I was so happy my baby was a boy.

Let me sidetrack for a moment. I couldn't get fully excited. Prior to having our baby, family let me down big time. There was a lack of support and someone broke the family village code. I cried for help to them, yet no one could hear me. I guess this is normal family behavior in the black family. When someone cries for help, we tell him or her to rough up or nothing is wrong with you. Then, if there are signs of mental health issues, they are considered crazy for lashing out. All things can trigger us.

So, let me get back on topic of why I appreciate any and every woman who has decided to be a stay at home mom.

It was time for me to take my baby home, and settle in. Big brother, Kourtney, and big sister, Kori, welcomed baby Kobi home with open arms.

A month passed, and for some reason, I could not adjust myself to stay at home with three kids while my husband was at work five days a week. I thought this was going to be easy, but as the days grew longer, my mind was a nervous wreck.

My every day, stay at home mom, routine: baths, bottles, naps, clean, prepare kids for school and break up kid fights. Sometimes, I had little or no sleep what so ever, and would forget to eat.

I was worried, I was confused, I was drained, I was sad, I was scared and I was nervous. Why did I feel this way? I experienced many changes, both physically and mentally. My mood was all over place. This happened during the postpartum stages. I felt weird and disordered, and just did not know what to do. The feelings were terrifying! I didn't think anyone would understand or listen to me without judging what I was facing.

I thought about what people would say, "You decided to have your kids, and have to take care of them." The opinion overwhelmed me. Yet, I needed to be strong for my family. I could not let my family see me down. My children needed me, and my husband had to go to work. He provided for our family, and I didn't want him worried about my drama. Anyway, he may have believed that I was complaining and not trying. I didn't want to let down my family and had to figure another way out. I had to come up with a plan, and fast.

First step, I decided to create a plan of action with steps that had clears goals and were measureable and attainable. I looked for a physician and therapist and identified them as my support team. These are things I was never taught to do.

I was missing a key thing that individuals need in life, self-care. I didn't know how to take good care of myself, my mental and physical health.

I hit rock bottom. Didn't know I needed help so badly. I was diagnosed with severe postpartum and mental illness disorders.

I was confused as ever and never concerned about my mental health before. I was having a mental breakdown.

I feared anyone thinking that my condition was a black woman's pity party. It was not! I didn't want other people's attention. I was a black woman, who had been strong for so long and had reached her breaking point. My hormones were out of control. I kept trying to figure out how do I get back normal? I really wanted help.

I worked with my physician, therapist, and God. They helped me figure it all out. I had overthought everything.

Either by choice or circumstance, I had faced a new normal. I accepted help was need, and decided to do whatever work necessary until I was healed from what was making me overthink and feel like the lifestyle I chose was wrong for me.

I changed the people around me, and didn't give energy to past situations that was experienced by in a long time ago. I no longer covered up my hurt.

It was my time to be healed, and to stop thinking and questioning negatively about myself.

As time went on, I decided to get baptized. It cleared my path for a new start and cleansed my dirty soul. I was damaged and needed major repair. I had to better for my husband, my beautiful children, and myself, and set clear specific goals for success.

I was gifted a red journal to write down my life dreams, goals and passion. It was time for Micai to start taking good care of Micai, and focus on moving forward.

Sitting in the house as a stay at home mom was much needed. It was giving me a chance to reflect on my past experiences. Taking time to reflect was allowing me to figure out what is really important to me. What was really important at that point was doing for me.

My whole life, I was doing so much for other people, and never took the chance to see what I love to do or what I wanted to do for myself. I had the ability to do great things, but those abilities turned into other people's things.

Flawed Mom

In my household, everyone's needs were met from doctor's appointments to parent-teacher conferences. I had to remember all those things, and make it work. After a while, it was too demanding.

Finally, I had to reach my own full potential. Were the steps hard? The answer is yes. Did I doubt my ability to mother and be a good wife? The answer is yes. It was a struggle, but I kept pushing myself to be more successful, the person God envisioned me to be.

All that I had encountered, I had inner strength and was more resilient. I had to stop complaining, and start making better moves.

I still needed help. I was still tired of myself. I was still looking at the things, and people around me that caused me drama and mess.

My energy was so important to me at this point. I had to remove myself from situations and people, but I didn't know how.

I asked God to help remove those that didn't serve no purpose in my life and not trying to help better me, bring me down and make me feel bad for doing what's meant for me, didn't respect me, and didn't understand my need to growth. I cried out to God in time of my urgent need.

This was truly my chance to start fresh. I wasn't letting anyone stop my mission.

As my mind started to expand, I started to see my light shine. I started to realize how I could be a light in my darkness, and the light in my family and friend's life.

I deserved my family and friends light, and they deserved mine. My plan could work for all of us. I had to take massive action, go to work on myself. I had to be the best Micai could be without hesitation.

I had to see my therapist and keep up with appointments. This was a must, a priority, and a system that had to be done consistently.

I wanted this healing more than even before. I felt like recovery was my last thing to do on earth. The trauma, the hurt, and the guilt were slowly draining my life away, and I wanted to release the painful memories and emotions that were stored in my body.

It was time to start investing in me financially and mentally. I decided to get into the business of spiritual healing, a connection to something greater than oneself-to heal others and myself. It is a higher power or some sense of higher truth, beauty or sacredness in life.

This is what I believed my calling was and I was ready. Will my family support me? Will they listen to my ideas? Will this made sense to anyone?

My husband told me that I have his full support and that's all that mattered. But, in reality, was I looking for encouragement from my entire family? Yes, I was. Writing this chapter, I realized my family was my main obstacles and problems. They were my trigger.

Family is very important to me, means so much to me. But, the level of needing their support, my opinion and experience, is hopeless and disturbing. I have the kind of family that thinks you already got it. They refuse to let you get ahead of them and use you to support them with no reciprocity.

So, guess what? I have no room for family anymore at this point. I love them from a distance. Family has resided with me. I helped them raise their kids, and did everything to make sure they were comfortable. When it was my turn, they turned their backs on me. At first, I didn't understand it, but now I do.

Being a stay at home mom allows me a much-needed break, and the family to function better. I am able to spend time with my husband, my children, and myself at home. But, sometimes you want to plan a date night away from home.

Occasionally, I have asked family to help out with my kids, and they replied, "I'm busy." None of my family members are married, so they wouldn't understand why date nights matter. My husband and I knew already our families expected response. We realized our date nights are a necessity, and would find a way to make things happen with no exceptions and no excuses. It would be just like the good ole days for us.

I've done all the right things to raise my family. My husband and I have made sacrifices, and we had to be strong for each other and our kids. This is our little family, and we are doing the best we can do.

I sat and thought about what is the value of a stay at home mom, where do I start with my family goals, how do I create an amazing schedule for my family, and how do I keep my family connected, and how do we fit in time to communicate as a family? Then, I considered me. How do I adjust or change? How do I get started to become?

First, I had to figure out what I really wanted to do with my life and without missing my kid's events. I had goals to start my own women organizations. I wanted a book club, a transitional living program, and a resource center. I desired to help women, and knew it would take hard work, time, and dedication, and still be a stay at home mom.

Many people asked, "Why are you doing so much," and stated, "You are not going to be able to do them all." I refused to let their words discourage me. I thought about everything that had been done for others with my assistance, all I wanted to accomplish for me. I had to become an entrepreneur. The more I heard their words, the more determined I was to set and achieve my goals right away.

I had never shown any dedication to myself, and for once I was going to do what I actually wanted. I wasn't going to give up now, never.

I decided to start doing women empowerment seminars and events to gain a following. I started to work side jobs to invest in my dreams. I wanted to get more involved with community work, so I volunteered to help others. I got so involved. I became addicted to doing the work, to be a part of it all. I was relieved to a part of something.

I was more than a wife, a mom, and a go to person. I was a servant leader.

Still, I help people, but doing it my way makes me feel happy and appreciated. The persons who receive help from me show so much respect. It feels great to help my community get to the next level.

My three-year-old son is a very busy baby. This is a new experience because none of my other kids were like him at all. My patience has run short after this last birth, and I don't understand why. I know all kids are different, but I can't keep up with his adventurous life. He has an attitude of curiosity.

I get frustrated a lot and can't fight my irritation, unwanted anger. I have isolated myself from everyone to calm my nerves.

Why is my child so hyper? At this point, I don't want any more kids. He is a two-year-old boy. Is that the problem? I don't know the reason, but I have a loss of patience. Is it still postpartum depression? I don't know how long it lasts. Some research shows after three years.

Lately, I'm talking to my therapist, writing in my journal, and keeping busy with the women organizations. Being around others in my Woman's Worth Book Club is helping to release a lot of stress. I am moving forward.

Balancing the life of the Easley's is not an easy task, ever. But, we're making adjustments, every now and then, so no one in the house feels neglected.

I look forward to slow days. Some days are rough and other days are smooth. On the smooth days, I am able to relax.

I make sure my kids are involved in school activities and events, birthday invites, and much more. However, timing is everything in life. Especially, when you are dealing with mental illness and parenting. It is hard to be the parent you want to be, by I am raising my kids to be strong and to have the courage and confidence to reach their full potential. I receive a lot of community support.

My kid's environment is healthy, and they attend good schools. Definitely, they get the proper knowledge.

The sacrifices that my husband I make to take care of our kids are for their and our good, a better life. We chose to live in reduced violent crime and peace disturbance neighborhoods, and our needs over our wants to make us better parents and our children safe and happy.

I never imagined a family of five. It all seemed not so real. I knew God blessed my family and me.

Just about everyone wants to be married with kids. It requires work. You have to find a balance between married life and raising kids. It's not about you. Consider patience and time too. Work hard, have resources, and connect with people who have a genuine willingness to help you. Stop worrying and get confident. Concentrate on a happy, healthy family. Become the best version of yourself.

You may lose people, including family, when you start embracing yourself and winning at life. You are good. Stay focus and don't make your journey about anyone else. Trust me, you got this. You may not know this, but your life is being elevated to success and abundance right now.

I have a wonderful husband that supports my kids and me to his best ability, and we appreciate him so much for loving us. He bought us our first home, and continues to set goals with the family in mind.

My husband invested in all of my dreams, and motivates me to dream bigger.

I stay busy with six businesses: Woman's Worth Book Club, Worthy Girls Book Club, Worthy Boys Book Club, Pure Pearl Wellness Spa, Enjoli Woman Transitional Living, and of course my collaboration with Flawed Mom Too. I am a co-author in the book, a doula to pregnant women during their labor, and a mom entrepreneur who inspires other mothers.

I got this, and I am not giving up on my dreams to be a stay at home mom. I do this for my family. I'm a fabulous mom who sets boundaries for my family.

All I need at this point is to attract positive energy and raise my positive vibrations. Feeling good and healing are all that matters.

Micai Easley

6 THE NEW WIFE

I never thought I would get married to my ex-boyfriend. It's crazy to say, "I'm Mrs. Polk." Never in a million years, would I have thought that at all.

I'm somebody's wife. I have to listen, obey, and remember the vows I took. I know marriage is a process. It takes time for both parties to understand and learn to continue to have a success, healthy, and happy marriage.

I'm a wife that's still learning to understand a person I've known for twenty plus years. I'm not perfect and I make mistakes, but my husband accepts me for who I am and loves me unconditionally.

Sometimes you don't know a person until you live with them in your household. Okay!

My husband proposal wasn't the usual on one knee. It was through a homemade Valentine's Day card since we were broke. It said, "Happy first eee-yip Valentines!" Inside the card states, "Roses are red, violets are blue, and Polk is my last name can I make it yours too?"

I thought it was the cutest thing ever. We didn't have a date planned, and he just kept telling me that it would happen soon. I'm like, okay!

Before we took the vows, we found out that we were pregnant. It was beyond shocking to me because of the 28 years of my life I've never been pregnant. But, here he comes along and I get knocked up.

Months later, we got hit with some bad news at the doctors' appointment that changed our relationship and brought us closer than before. We had a miscarriage with our first child together. That was the hardest thing in my life I could experience. To hear a doctor utter those words out her mouth could kill my soul.

My husband never left my side. I had pain and surgery, and he was there to give me comfort and moral support.

I cried for two months, and didn't want to go around anybody. I thought the loss of our child was my fault. I questioned God, and wanted to know if it was something wrong with me, what did I do wrong to have to deal with the pain of losing Truth?

In the experience, I knew that my bond with my husband was forever true. He told me that my pain was his pain. He had to be even stronger for me.

If I didn't have a child, my husband would be okay with the choice and still would love me.

Slowly, but surly, he helped me to get out of the deep, dark depression I was going through. We decided to wait a year to conceive another child. After the complicated grief, I was okay with our decision because I couldn't take another disappointment.

I felt like it was my fault overall and I couldn't do anything to fix it. I had to make it through my life's change and transition my mind into something else to ease my pain.

It was time to plan a wedding! I didn't have a big, fairy tale wedding. My husband told me that he wanted to do something intimate first, but knew I desired a big wedding. I was okay with what he wanted. We planned everything out and changed a couple of things along the way.

On the day of my wedding, it rained and nothing seemed to go as planned. I needed car brakes service, and had make-up and hair appointments.

My husband figured everything out for me. He called me an Uber driver to be on time for my make-up appointment. He even informed me that my car was repaired and parked around the corner if I had my key to drive.

I was set. I had to get a quick hairstyle, done by my cousin, and then go get dressed. Time wasn't my best friend and I was beyond late. But, I arrived to the wedding ceremony. It crossed my mind that this would be the last time I would be known as Swayze Marie Jackson.

All I could think about was this is finally happening today. There was no turning back. There I was walking hand in hand up these steps with this man. This was it, and the only person who can stop me is I. I had no reason to stop.

Here it goes, our vows were given and rings were presented. Then, I heard the pastor say, "You are now, Mr. and Mrs. Polk. You may kiss now."

We signed the marriage certificate, and our marriage is legal and valid. I didn't feel any different after getting married a minute ago.

But once he put a picture on social media and it went viral, I felt excited and married. Some people thought it was a joke and others screenshot the picture and sent it to me or other people. I got so many phone calls from people who asked if our marriage was a joke.

I sent family members pictures to let them know about the change in my life. I had started a new journey. My best friend even called me and went off on me because he talked to me all day and I didn't say anything to him at all. I had people mad because I didn't let them know to come.

I had to tell people, this was not our big wedding. It

was an intimate ceremony between husband and wife. "Awe, okay," is what I got from people.

I had people mad because they didn't know. My own family didn't know what we were doing. I didn't even tell them.

At the end of the day, I can say I made the best choice for my happiness and me. What is for me is for me and nobody else, but my husband. My husband and I are not giving anybody permission to say we made the wrong choice. It was for us.

I know a lot of people had their opinions and judged us about our wedding ceremony. May 18, 2018, was a day just for my husband and me, and we will always remember and cherish it.

I'm just saying, "The entire St. Louis knows what it is." LOL. Mr. and Mrs. Polk was a big, shocking announcement.

A lot of people didn't recognize me on most of the pictures that my husband posted. Some looked at us in the images and said that they'd known us for many years and would have never thought we'd be married to each other. That is so crazy to me!

Some think our marriage is a fairy tale, others think it is matrimony. For me, it's a blessing in disguise for someone to come back into your life years later.

God gave me happiness when I didn't even know it. He showed me that my husband has always been there. I just didn't know it, but God did. No matter how many trials and tribulations a woman will face, a door will always open for you.

Listen. Let me tell you how marriage has been for me one and a half year in the game. My husband and I do everything together. It's okay with us because we have fun together, and are in love. We have a happy and fulfilling life together.

There are times that we spend apart as well, but most times we are together. Our marriage is meaningful to us. We are a single unit, and genuinely appreciate each other as separate individuals.

It's not in my nature to be with someone every day. However, I enjoy becoming with my husband, loving more and more each day. We are in the beginning of our forever life together and have a desire to share activities and pursuits.

The beginning of a marriage can be very hard because there are a lot of things to learn with each other. We are learning to offer comfort and concern, and have a positive effect on each other.

My grandmother raised me. I have a high level of well-being, and high expectations. To me, it is important to treat other people and their property with respect, pick up after yourself, make amends when you hurt someone, and tell the truth.

I hate a mess, dirty stuff, and asking a person to help me. If I have to sound like a broken record, say the same thing over and over again, then stuff doesn't get done promptly. I wait to see if my husband will meet my expectation. If he doesn't, I snap then do it myself.

I've been doing stuff on my own for so long that at times it's hard for me to depend on another person to help me out. I know it is okay to depend on my husband. So I ask for help and expect him to take over responsibility. If he doesn't, then it is war, and I'm going off on him.

I have a dependent personality, and need to work on my attitude and anger because they both are messed up. I can get so mad. Sometimes I tell my husband to leave me alone. Other times I tell him to go about his business and hang with his friends.

There are times that I think he gets on my nerves. Then, I can say hurtful things. I don't like it when I ask my husband for help and don't get it. Especially, if he spends all his time on social media like the world is about to end.

I ask married women for help with managing my marriage. I want to hear from married women who deal with similar situations and want to strength their marriage, too. They tell me that men don't get what we are saying, and can be slow. Too, a wife has to break down the requests so husbands will understand.

Now, I feel like you can't teach old dogs new tricks. It's often difficult to get people to do things differently, especially if they've done it a certain way for so long. To me, I believe if you've with any woman before, you should know household expectations, stuff.

Everything is very simple to me. If I need help to keep housework from hurting our marriage, then help me husband. Let's try to do better. Or a baby, that's not going to happen in no shape or form.

I can get on his nerves like he does mine. But in a marriage, it's about compromise at all times. Yes, people can see us on social media and see us having a good time, but always there is another side to what we got going on.

At times, I get tired of people calling for my husband and me to join them at an event. He is ready, and goes out the door while telling me that he's about to go do this or that.

I'm not asking my husband to be all over me all of the time because he is overly affectionate. But, I'd life for us to do something small together rather than in groups. After a while, I tell him to go about his business. I'll just jam on my own in the house or wherever. I know how to be alone and not be bothered by anyone.

Our second pregnancy, I felt alone in the marriage. I didn't want to do much or hang out around people. I couldn't drink alcohol or smoke hookah so why go out with people who enjoy that only. All I could do was sit in the space and use my cell phone as entertainment.

There were many times, I cried to myself and pulled myself together. I had to be strong for our child.

During the pregnancy, I did a lot of shopping for the kid and going to doctor appointments while still doing my household responsibilities. I'm so independent. I just did what I had to do.

Once my daughter arrived, going through labor and delivery, I felt alone in the hospital. My husband was there with me, but he was sleeping and snoring. He told me that he was going to take off work the next day, already approved, but he went to work.

I was at home in pain, and sometimes no help. Other times, my mother helped. But, I physically or emotionally, I didn't have a baby with my mother. I was depressed.

Often, I thought about how was he with his other children and their mothers. I shouldn't felt this way in the marriage, but I did.

There was a lot of stuff that my husband didn't get or want to get, didn't help me with or want to help me with. We discussed this over and over again. He believed things were positively happening, but I thought opposite. I tried to control my emotions so my emotions didn't control me.

Don't get me wrong. Whatever I want, my husband makes a way to get it for me. But, marriage emotions and real-life feelings, we need to work on more. There are times, I told him that I'd put our daughter first, before him because I don't feel like he puts me first. Too, he had to get more situations under control. I wanted to separate myself from him, and I was okay with it.

A lot of people say, "Happy wife, happy life." If only our husbands could understand that 100% of the time. I have my flaws and my husband does too. We are both total opposites though.

My husband is a non-confrontational person so he won't say anything when we disagree. He walks away or finds something to do other than address our issue.

Me on the other hand, I'm going to keep expressing myself because I cannot get over a situation without holding a conversation about it. Once a person pushes my buttons, it is war. As a married woman I have learned to let things go. Everything isn't about me, and isn't worth a fight.

My husband is patient with me. If he didn't love all of me, then he wouldn't have married me. Marriage is not compatible.

If people in the marriage have the privilege to come and go as he or she pleases, then they should be considered friends with benefits.

I vowed to be with my husband for the rest of my life. I chose to honor and obey him.

My husband knows everything about me. He's willing to fix anything and everything right or wrong for me. He's my protector.

We are in the beginning stages of our marriage, but it

seems as if we've been doing this forever.

I love exposing new things to my husband, and that he is choosing to do and see them with me. We are taking our time to learn about each other's interest and concerns, and enjoying everything about it. After all, we are spending the rest of our lives together.

My husband and I do not compare our marriage to any other married couple because nobody's marriage is the same. There are similarities and differences in marriages, but everyone has to discover how to work together in the marriage rather than out the marriage, unless it is an expert, to build a great marriage. We face common issues such as laziness, household expectations, and whatever else that spark our arguments. The larger concerns, like I mentioned before, should be discussed with an expert who can help us and not married couples who can hurt us.

As a new wife, I'm taking on a role that everybody cannot handle. I keep on my big girl panties to deal with multiple situations. I'm a woman that wears multiple hats, and can take on any task that's presented to me. Some things I can do in a snap of a finger and other things might take me some time.

As a new wife, I am my husband's biggest supporter, cheerleader, backbone and more. I have learned the roles and responsibilities in marriage are different for a husband and a wife. I am willing to do anything possible to have a truly happy marriage.

Marriage is about love. My husband pisses me off at times, but he makes me smile and laugh. He loves me beyond measures.

What could be better than being married to Mr. Polk? He's no famous rapper, songwriter or activist, he he's all I need and more. He's an outgoing, energetic, loving party animal.

Marriage is more than saying I do, it's a union of two soul mates embracing memories of everlasting love and happiness. Until I get pissed off. LOL. I'm just playing.

Swayze Polk

7 THE ENTREPRENEUR MOM

Being an entrepreneur mom can be the hardest thing to do. I began managing it all in winter 2015.

I was standing on the assembly line at General Motors, waiting to install a handle on the driver's seat. I had a worker on both sides of me, each one of us assigned a specific task. The seat was coming, and I was getting ready to do my part. While working, I was daydreaming, which wasn't unusual. I was good at doing my job, which was happening in 35 seconds instead of the one-minute that was required. Thinking about how fast I was working, producing 400 seats in an 8-hour day, for someone else business. Right then, I began imagining how to start, run, and grow my own business, and remembering my ability to make other people smile and feel confident about them. I loved it!

I had attended dental school in past years, but worked on an assembly line for 8 hours a day. I stood there thinking is this really what I want to do for the rest of my life? My opinions, beliefs, and goals crossed my mind, but seemed not to matter. I worked as a well-paid robot. At the time, I had two children and a husband at home. Plus I had bills and a care note to pay. I felt trapped. I had to stay because of my 8-hour job benefits: reward me financially and competitively, support my family, and provide a routine schedule.

One day, I reported to work and discovered a decision had been made to move me to another station. It made me very angry because I was comfortable in my position on the assembly line at station seven. The production line leaders knew this too. They saw proficiency in my ability to perform the tasks required to do on the assembly line, and qualities of a good worker (team-oriented, positive attitude, dependable, strong work ethic).

Finally, I realized that I am an employee, not an employer. I understood the employer could transfer me whenever and wherever. I was just an operator who built seats, not an owner of a multinational corporation. My opinion didn't matter, and I didn't call any shots on the job. All I could do was continue to have a good employee benefits package and a weekly paycheck.

I had been employed at General Motors for two plus years, and operated like an assembly line robot for them. I demonstrated production speed and consistency, but it did not matter.

Spring 2016, one beautiful day, I wrote down clear, personal goals to help shape my life the way I want it to be. The list included everything that I loved to do.

The thought crossed my mind that I had graduated high school, and worked as a promoter. A position I really liked. I handed out flyers, attended special events, and met popular celebrities. I enjoyed the perks of being a promoter, and got an adrenaline rush from doing the work. It all felt good. I wanted that same feeling again. But, how could I do what I love and love what I am doing and be happy?

Then, I thought about my dental trade again, and how I didn't want the experience to be a waste. I had been top of my class. I asked myself, "How could I turn it into a business, something I really love?"

First step was to get out my personal goal list, and consider my children's needs. I had student loans and other bills to think about too. I began with the list that included my vision.

Next, I started putting money aside every pay period,

and looking at my goal list every day to become stronger, happier, and more effective. I realized that it was going to require a lot of hard work and faith.

I admired a lot of women who had become mom entrepreneurs, and said, "I can do this too!" I wanted to be well known and more important for something. It seemed easy to be a 9-to-5, average working mom. I wanted to be challenged without hesitation, and weighed the pros and cons. Then, I decided to take the risk.

I talked to my children about my goals and plan to create My Celebrity Smile, a mobile teeth-whitening business with products to obtain the highest quality of oral hygiene. They were excited. Spring 2016, my dream happened, came true.

I knew the dream would require sacrifices. There were days, weeks, and months I wouldn't get my hair and nails done because I needed to buy school clothes and dental products, and pay bills. I stopped eating out at restaurants and taking my lunch to work. I believed the bigger the sacrifice, the bigger the reward.

My mother was who inspired me. She owned a nail salon while I attended high school. I continued to sacrifice, and eventually my dreams had become my reality.

My suggestion, invest everything into your own business. Visualize yourself accomplishing what you believe. It will happen, something my mom always told me. Have your family support, especially a significant other or spouse because you share responsibility. However, be any means, be happy and make your dreams come true.

I went into business with no support from my significant other. If God gives you a vision, He will help you overcome struggles. Trust Him. It was hurtful dealing with an unsupportive person that I thought was with me through it all. But, God honored me, and I embraced Him. I prayed and everything worked out.

Sometimes your vision is not for everyone and everybody. Think about the big picture (results) to achieve specific goals, determine acceptable levels of support, and then create to make results happen. My business was created for my children and me. I wanted us to have something we could call our own.

I knew most millionaires became successful by inheritance and investments. I wanted this for my children because I didn't come from wealth. I knew from that day forward, I had to be disciplined and consistent. I was determined to break the barriers and strong grips that were holding me back life.

I dreamed of whitening well-known individuals and celebrities.

I was charismatic and strong-minded. I wanted it all for my family. I believed that I would walk the red carpet and embrace celebrities. And the day that it happened for me, I knew that my dream had become my reality. I met the nicest celebrities, and the rudest, arrogant celebrities.

I started this business with no brick and mortar. I would setup my mobile teeth-whitening business at events and popup shops. I used other people business, to make my business work. I learned how to build good working relationships with customers and colleagues, appreciate others, be positive and on my best behavior. At the end of the day, I had created mutually beneficial outcomes.

I graduated dental school, and had become a mobile

dental technician for several dentists. I took my skills and ran with them.

As a dental technician for other dentists, I had been mistreated, overworked, underpaid, and underrepresented as a minority and a woman in the dentistry field. For a period, couple of years, I left dentistry due to a lack of diversity and inclusion in the workplace.

I made a side-by-side comparison of my experience as a dental technician and a production worker, and found similar issues. That was it. I wanted my own business. I continued to work full-time as a production worker, and my part-time job as an entrepreneur. At this point, I had nothing to lose, everything to gain.

I had a vision, a strong desire, and a clear intention. I aligned my actions with my goals. I sacrificed by starting my own business. There were days that I had to pay people to watch my children while I traveled just to whiten teeth.

How did I get clients to come to my business? I had to partner with other businesses or to take my business to clients, mostly celebrities. Most times, I had to go where my customers were, which meant a job could be 30-minutes away in the same city or 12-hours away in a different city. I would travel by car, which mean the drive time was the same in both directions in one day of work. Yet, I increased my visibility. I met different types of people, and it gave me great exposure for my business.

Honestly, being an entrepreneur mom is no the easiest thing to do. There are days that you will not make money at all, and get discouraged. On those days, you have to find ways to supplement your income, especially if you are transitioning from a day job to start your own business. Then, there are days that you will make money and see quitting your job to start your own business was the best thing you ever did.

As an entrepreneur, you will probably do odd jobs other than usual. I delivered food, worked at an assembly line factory, cleaned houses, sold unwanted items, and the list continues.

I recommend you get a sponsor to support your vision. It will make the process much easier.

Keep your vision in front of you. I continue to honor God, and work with Him to set goals and achieve my dreams.

As a business owner, whitening teeth and delivering smiles is what I do. I make it all happen with no exceptions and no excuses. Those who stand for nothing fall for everything. I stand on God promises through my shortcomings.

I continue to grow and learn every day. There is still a lot of work to do, which requires sleepless nights. But, I survive the days because I see visiting other countries in my future.

I am forever grateful to have my children who love me unconditionally. My children have been my number one supporter. In fact, my daughter is co-owner of My Celebrity Smile, and she plans to become an orthodontist. I am happy they have seen my elevation and me do anything I put my mind, too.

Always, I keep in mind the reason My Celebrity Smile was created, and embrace the world with my gift. Being an entrepreneur mom is part of my path that God has for me, and I am thankful to Him. I will not trade what He has allowed under no circumstances.

The meaning of being flawed is imperfect in some way or character or not containing mistakes. I understand that every day in life it is never perfect, but I will continue to strive for greatness, daily. I am the executive of My Celebrity Smile; and I will work to grow this business and shift the smile industry into greatness!

Diana Bonner

Flawed Mom

I've almost never been on time for anything. I think I'm a baby blamer. Since my kids are older, I know for sure that I shouldn't be all extra getting them prepared, but I blame them anyway for my tardiness. I don't think any business would accept or appreciate that so I never had plans on working a regular job. Clocking in and out would kill my income. I am a full-time mom of five so being broke is not an option.

I'm married, and my husband earns a very decent income, but two is obviously better than one. I just can't see myself sitting around letting my brain go to waste. I love that I am able to provide for my family. I remember being in a situation where I wasn't able to provide and that left me feeling like crap. My babies deserve way better than that, so do my husband and I.

My life isn't just based off of wanting to be available for my children at all times. I'm also happy to be able to work doing what I love. I couldn't imagine having to do something every day that didn't make me happy or where I couldn't make others happy because I'm not passionate or have no love for the type of work I'm doing. I get distracted easily when I'm not interested in what's in front of me, I may even fall asleep.

I tried working a job when I was in 11th grade, and at ages 19 and 21. I think that working at a shoe store, up the street from my house, was the longest time I worked and I don't think that was a full calendar year.

Each tax season, I worked as a tax preparer from 2008 to present. You're probably thinking that's a seasonal job. Well that's considered a traditional job for me because I went to work and earned an income for my family. The last time I worked for a tax company was in 2017. Since then, tax preparation is a service that I provide as a small business owner.

I have always wanted to be available for my children, no matter what. If their school calls, then the teacher and my child will see me shortly. I take my babies to practice, pick them up, and make any and every doctor's appointment, school meetings, you know the normal stuff that I could possibly miss if I had to go to work for someone else. This is the life that I chose and this is what works for me.

People may think it's easy to work from home and maintain a household, but my life is far from simple. It has taken patience, consistency, and determination to work for myself.

The hardest part about being a stay at home mom is remembering to have a life outside of my home. I have no complaints because I'm living the life that I prayed for.

However, I'm always thinking what will be next for me. I'm comfortable to a degree. I appreciate everything that I have because I worked hard for it.

I have not lied, cheated, or stole from anyone to obtain the level of success that I have. That may sound easy also, but it's not and where I am from it's not really normal.

Most of the people I know have committed some type of illegal activity to become financially free. Then they are able to live an entrepreneur life. No shade to anyone doing anything his or her heart desires, but I take pride in being honest and hard working. Not to mention I don't owe one person a dime, not even my life partner. I have put my blood, sweat, and tears into working from home for myself. It's a damn good feeling.

I've made plenty of mistakes on my entrepreneurial journey. Thank God. I have learned from them all and can honestly say that I haven't made the same mistakes more than once. I've also been able to share my experiences with family, friends, and associates so that other moms who are entrepreneurs won't experience the same struggles I have.

Consistency is the number one thing that has helped me to be able to keep my bills paid. The passion that I have for working with women and children, who want to be their own bosses, is my reason for success. They are my why.

Last year, my daughters became entrepreneurs and they have been on a roll. They've had numbers of interviews and speaking engagements due to their success. The girls are ages 10, 11, and 12, and they have made enough money to fund anything that they want to do. They've earned enough to pay their own bills.

In 2013, I started selling t-shirts. I'll never forget how excited I was to receive my first package. I hired a graphic designer that I met on social media. She provided a print service as well. The graphic designer came up with three designs, and sent me about three versions of each. I selected the designs that I fell in love with and waited about two weeks to receive them in the mail. It was on.

I participated in fashion shows and vendor events. I

even hosted my own pop up shops that were very successful. I met so many other entrepreneurs, and that's what helped me to create a buzz.

I launched an online store shortly after and started to sell women's shoes also. I got a small office in a professional building downtown St. Louis that ran me somewhere under $400, all utilities included. At the office, I spent all day and night brainstorming, taking pictures of models and working extra hard. It was like my second home, some nights I slept there.

In 2015, I hosted my very first fashion show, produced by my bonus dad who had produced shows all over the world for different networks and elite companies. I hired a whole team, and we did so well that everyone was paid that night, even my bonus dad. I had a producer, host, model coordinator, sound technician, light technician, and hair stylist. I'm sure that I left out a title, but there were plenty of us that came together to put that show together. The models, stylist and designers were amazing! It felt so good to do what I loved!

I relocated from St. Louis, my hometown, to Houston in 2015. I operated my own online store and my daughter's too.

My daughters and I were so busy with attending pop ups and vendor events that people would randomly hit us up to be a part of trade shows, radio shows, speaking engagements, vendor events and whatever else you could think of to expose our brands. I met people from all walks of life.

I can't believe some of the rooms I've been in or the prominent people that I have rubbed shoulders with just based off my daughters and I selling t-shirts. The key to our success is consistency and perseverance.

I am a mother first, and an entrepreneur second. I have been under pressure as both, but nothing in this world can change the fact that my heart desires to be the best at both.

It gives me butterflies every time I think about where my family will be in 6, 9, or 12 months from now. My family is my motivation and my backbone. If we are not together at an obligation or a commitment, rest assure that whoever is not present, he or she is at another engagement that our empire will benefit from.

My family and I are all business partners, and have multiple businesses. It is a luxury to have members of my household as my right hand man. I thank God daily for the opportunity.

Amber Farrar

8 THE MOTHER WHO BURIED HER CHILD

No mother should ever have to bury her child or no mother should never outlive their children are both sayings that I have heard many times in my lifetime.

Life as we know it happens and events take place that is out of our control. How do you stop worrying about things you have no control over? How do you deal with things we can't prevent or prepare for, things we never thought could happen?

On October 21, 2018, I became a mother who had to bury my son Rashaad Lamarr Bobbitt, something no mother should ever have to do. I did it, and it was the most devastating moment in my life.

My name is Chinara Meeks. I am 31-years-old, single mother of two children. My youngest son, Rashaad Bobbitt, was taken from me unexpected in 2008 due to gun violence in a drive-by shooting.

On October 21, 2008, I remember my family caught in the crossfire of a drive-by shooting while in a car. Rashaad was the only person in the car that was shot. He was shot one time in the back of his head. It all happened so fast.

I wish I could erase this painful memory, but I remember this day so vividly. My oldest son Kevin Coleman, who is now 15-years-old, was also in the car and witnessed his little brother get shot in the head. My baby Rashaad was shot only one time, but the one time was a fatal shot. I remember holding him until the ambulance showed up, watching his life leave his body, and feeling as if I was dying there with him.

I know this is a lot to read, but it would only be real if I shared my whole experience. I struggled with sharing my story in detail, but this is a part of who I am and it's a part of my testimony that needs to be heard. So, I'm fearlessly sharing my story raw and uncut.

I remember riding in the ambulance on what seemed like the longest ride ever. I remember the woman ambulance driver hugging me. I remember being alone at the hospital and the chaplain coming to pray with me. Things were moving so fast and my life was changing before my very eyes. My son died on that day at St. Louis Children's Hospital. I felt like a part of me died too on that day.

I have been a mother for half of my life. I remember falling in love with both of my children the minute I found out I was pregnant with them. I believe I can speak for most mothers when I say, "I fell in love with my child even when he or she was just a thought." We don't have to know what they look like, who they are going to be, or how they will love us. We just love them from the start.

I think it's amazing that before even knowing a person you can love them unconditionally. My love for my sons ignited a fire in me that at the time I couldn't comprehend. Motherhood will do that to you.

A mother should never have to bury her child. Being a mother, I understand the severity and weight of that statement. We shouldn't outlive a life that we are supposed to have so many plans for, so many promises to keep and fulfill. But, life brought me to this traumatic moment in my life.

I am a mother who did what a mother should never have to do. I outlived my child and had to bury him. Even though this tragedy had changed the course of my life, I knew I had Kevin and I had to find the strength and courage to be there for him. I knew he was depending on me in so many ways, and couldn't let him down even though I felt life had let me down.

I felt so guilty about Kevin's pain. He didn't deserve to watch his brother pass and he didn't deserve to endure the pain of losing a sibling. From the very beginning, I vowed to myself to make sure that Kevin's happiness was my top priority.

Although motherhood ignited a fire in me that I didn't comprehend, in this very moment I had a fire to find strength and courage in pain to get through and move forward for Kevin and myself.

Rashaad passed when he was only 17-months-old. I was 20-years-old, just some days before my 21st birthday and Kevin was 5-years-old at the time. So being a young mother, I had to figure out how to deal with grief after a traumatic loss, and how to heal from a trauma and move on. I wanted Kevin and my life to be normal.

Kevin was about to start kindergarten and I just wanted him to be a regular kid. I don't think I understood how he was affected by the trauma until we had so many different experiences in school. There were times in school when Kevin wouldn't know how to control his emotions, and he would act out and it showed up as anger.

I knew I had to create a support team for my son. Every year I met with his school counselor and his teacher of the grade he was attending to explain the events around the death of my son Rashaad. I made it my job to partner with his teachers because I didn't want him dealing with his pain alone, especially when I couldn't be around to console him. I never could've prepared for the things Kevin would go through as he grieved also. He would have an outburst at school because he didn't understand his emotions.

Thank God, I understood the power of creating a village for my son because teachers tried to understand his pain and they helped us through our loss. I took him to a counselor where we also learned tools to help him cope. I want to share the importance of allowing people to help you. I was able to create a support team for my son. It was work and sometimes I wanted to give up because I wanted him to be "normal," but I am thankful I didn't allow myself of getting in the way of creating our new normal.

I put all my power into helping my son heal. Putting your child first is what I believed a good mother should do.

I made it my biggest priority to ensure that he was a happy kid. I made it my goal to make sure that he overcame this loss. I didn't realize I was forgetting all about myself. I was just going through life hurting and not understanding my own pain.

We all go through hurts and disappointments in life, but to me, it seemed like things were magnified in my case. I had mastered smiling on the outside, but I felt as if I was screaming and no one could hear me. I didn't understand why I couldn't shake this feeling. I was working, raising my child, going out with family and friends, all at the same time I was dying inside.

My heart ached so badly. I knew I couldn't continue living like this. I took Kevin to a counselor and support groups, but I wasn't doing those things for myself. I knew how important a support team was for him, but I wanted to go through my pain alone. The reason I wanted to go through my pain alone is that the pain I felt hurt too bad and I didn't want anyone to hurt and feel the pain I did. So, I just continued through life not realizing I was self-destructing.

I didn't understand how my pain was steering the course of my life. As I reflect on my life, I didn't understand how much of a factor my pain was when I was getting into certain relationships or doing certain things. But, looking back I realize how a lot of my decisions were pain driven.

I partied a lot during this time. I think maybe this along with the choice of men were an outlet for me unknowingly. I didn't realize how much this lifestyle was draining me. I wasn't spending as much time with my son, Kevin, as I once did and it started showing in his behavior at school.

I went from wanting to create this new normal for my son to wanting to go to sleep and never waking up. I knew I had to shake this feeling because I couldn't imagine Kevin having to go through the loss of both his brother and his mother. I wanted to shake this feeling so badly, and decided I had to fight these feelings. I didn't know how I was going to fight, but I decided whatever I needed to do I would fight for both Kevin and myself. If I could do anything in my power it was to make sure my son never hurt again.

I know my healing had to be beyond what I could do myself. After Rashaad passed, I would have visitation dreams and connect with him. I remember the dreams would give me so much peace. I mention my dreams because I believe it was God's way of helping me heal. I would have these dreams or visitations all the time.

One dream I remember so vividly. I remember crying and being so sad in this dream, and hearing a voice talking so calmly to me. The voice was so soothing and gentle. The voice told me to allow my memories of my son to bring joy in my life. The voice told me to go through life and be somebody to others. I believe that was the voice of God. At the end of the dream, I remember holding my son who was dressed in all white and I was crying tears of joy. I believe this dream was an encounter to help push me into my destiny.

Now at the time, I didn't understand the dream, but had so much peace once I woke up. I guess that was a moment or an eureka moment, understanding an incomprehensible problem. From that moment, I knew I couldn't try to drain my pain away with wild living.

Now I am not saying enjoying yourself is bad. But, the way I was living, I know it wasn't my character. I was trying to mask my pain. From that moment on, when I started to feel sad, I would purposely cause myself to reflect on the memories of my son Rashaad. I would find myself laughing and smiling when I thought of him. Many times I would find myself thinking about the moments I spent teaching Rashaad his numbers and colors.

Rashaad only lived a short time, but it was like he knew so much. He could count to five and he knew all his body parts. I loved the memories of me teaching him.

Didn't realize how God was using my pain to propel me into my destiny. The memories I had of me teaching Rashaad and also my experience of creating a village with Kevin's teachers was the beginning push into my destiny of being a teacher. I knew I would be able to keep my son alive by helping families in my city the best way I knew how and that's by being a teacher.

My pain drove me to my purpose. I know the calling over my life of being a teacher is exactly where God wants me to be. In my city, I know many children have to endure the pain of losing someone. All too often, in St. Louis children have to go to school with the heavy burden of losing family members due to gun violence. It is so important that these children have people that understand their pain and know that they will make it out on the other side of their pain.

Losing my son Rashaad the way I did due to gun violence, I was so confused. He died so young and was taken so suddenly. His short-lived life lasted only 17 months, but made a huge impact in my heart. I refused to believe his physical death is the end to his life. He was so special and I know he would've done great things in the world.

I found myself always thinking about how I could create ways to keep Rashaad's name alive. It was amazing because the same time I was feeling this way, Kevin was always talking about his brother and feeling proud of him. Kevin was always giving credit to Rashaad. It was so astonishing for me to see Kevin growing through his grieving process.

As a family, Kevin and I create days to celebrate Rashaad's memories, which we do to this day. Kevin calls one of the days "Best Friends Day." We celebrate memories of Rashaad on the day he died instead of being sad. My whole family and my close friends participate. We don't do a big celebration, just make sure we all feel the love and presence of family and that we don't have to be sad alone. The love my family has for each other has helped us all as we continually healed from this tragedy. My family has grown so close after losing Rashaad. His death has taught us the importance of family and no matter what we love each other and are involved in each other's lives so much.

My story is a never-ending one. I believe throughout my life, I will continue to heal from the death of my son Rashaad in different ways.

The statement a mother should never bury their child

is one that I agree with. I wouldn't wish this type of pain on anyone, but I can encourage mothers who have to endure this pain. I can encourage them to do what they can to get through the discomfort.

For me, my pain has pushed me into my passion and purpose. My choice of healing is to keep Rashaad's name alive. The way I keep his name alive is by choosing to love and educate children in my city. I am currently a third-grade teacher and not only do I choose to teach my students academics I believe it is as important to teach them character and compassion. I try to teach as many children I come across the power of my love for them and the power that they have when they love others. I also let my students know that I am there for them, and when I know they have been through anything similar to what Kevin and I had to endure, I share Kevin's story with them and their parents and show them how resilience and perseverance can go along way and things will get better in life.

Losing my son Rashaad has taught me many things. One thing it has taught me is the power of forgiveness. Even though I am unaware of who caused this pain in the lives of my family and myself, I had to forgive whoever is responsible. I still have to explain the power of forgiveness to Kevin because I don't want him to go through life with the burden of unforgiveness. Another thing, Rashaad's death has taught me is the power of community.

I had to create a community for Kevin. I had to create a safe space for him to grieve. Through creating that safe space I watched him thrive and flourish through his pain. I also try to create that community for others because I know the power.

The power of love is another thing the death of my son

Rashaad has taught me. I know that love is the glue that continues to strengthen my family together and continues to help us heal.

My purpose for sharing something so near and dear to my heart is to show moms all around the world that you can make it. Burying a child is something a mother should never have to do, but I want to encourage you that if life brings you to it you can go through it. This is something I didn't choose to go through. But, I can say I chose to go through and not allow my pain to stop me. I chose to allow my pain to push me into my purpose. I allowed my pain to also dictate some choices that weren't the best too, but my mistakes have also made me the woman I am today.

I'm sharing in hopes that I can help someone not go through some of the things I went through while hurting. I want to encourage mothers everywhere not just mothers who have lost a child. Even though mothers who have gone through the same thing I've been through hold a special place in my heart.

I am so thankful I've been given this safe place to share my heart. I cried every time I sat down to share my story. I've told people my story, but I've never done it in writing and in the way of hoping to help someone heal from a loss in the ways that I have healed.

Chinara Meeks

9 THE SINGLE MOM

An American singer once said that life is a journey; every experience is here to teach you more fully how to be who you really are. I believe this statement is the difference between feeling like a single mom and being one.

One job I didn't expect is single parenting. I always wanted children, but never planned on being a single mom; however, it was planned for me. Yes, I was married when I had my son, but I divorced by the time he was five-years-old.

My divorce started during the unrest in Ferguson, MO, happenings that began the day after the fatal shooting of Mike Brown. I was afraid and frantic about raising a black son in St. Louis, MO, especially by myself.

The events surrounding Mike Brown's death heightened my fears and anxiety about raising an African-American male alone. Growing up, I always heard my grandmothers say that boys need their fathers, and as a seasoned educator, I felt that way as well.

I just could not believe God would do this to me after all the pain and long-term issues that come with growing up without my biological parents. I kept thinking wow, how much can I endure? Both of my parents were deceased by the time I was two-years-old, and my first two children died at birth. In my mind, this could not be possible; unfortunately, it was my reality.

Being a single mom, several times I cried, felt like a failure, and wanted my son to have more-something money couldn't buy, both parents in the home. Growing up, I was blessed to have four wonderful grandparents to raise me.

My maternal and paternal grandparents lived minutes

from each other. My aunts, uncles, and extended family were integral parts of my childhood. I realized in my adulthood, what a wonderful childhood I experienced. I was never abused physically or sexually, and was given an abundance of love and support from family and extended family. However, I was truly a daddy's girl, both of my grandfathers' baby.

Unfortunately, it still took years to ignore the absence of my parents. I remember as a child when I blew out my birthday candles each year, my wish was just to meet my parents for 5 minutes, not wanting to change anything about my childhood.

I lost my parents to the bitter drug war of the 70s; unfortunately, my father and mother were involved with a $30,000-day heroin trafficking ring. However, both parents were highly intelligent. My father skipped second grade, and my mother had an IQ two points from being a genius.

Now fast-forward, I am happy to say with my families' love and support, I am a success citizen and an educator. With my parent's intellect, I graduated Salutatorian of my high school class, securing me a four-year scholarship to a prominent university to become a math and science teacher.

Being a parentless child, it was major in my mind that I was being divorced and my son would not have his father in the home. I was deeply saddened by my divorce because I never wanted my son to experience the pain and sometimes loneliness I had endured being parentless. He doesn't deserve this, and I did everything right by the good book, so I thought. Why am I not being blessed?

During a dark moment, an epiphany occurred and my discernment became heightened. Only God could open my eyes to all the blessings that surrounded my son Peyton and I. Peyton is your blessing; you were 36-years-old with declining health and he was born healthy. God made me realize it is better to be from a broken home, than to have lived in one.

My family and friends quickly reminded me there is a job that has to be done and you have to do it if you are married or not. My sister from another mother raised an awesome African-American son without any help from his father.

My sister has been there for me since day, watching me endure postpartum depression and getting adjusted to motherhood. She is one of very few people that I take advice from, and she is still one of my biggest cheerleaders. My sister told me that a toxic mother is far worse than an absent father, so get out of my feelings. She said, "Passion, Look around you. Look at how blessed you are and your support system that includes your family, your bonus daughters, your ex-husband's first wife, and me." Yes, read it again, my ex-husband's first wife.

My ex-husband's first wife and I did not start as friends when he and I began to date. Her youngest daughter was nine-years-old. I understood he was divorced, but like other women in my situation I did not understand he was not finished with the marriage because they had children together.

As a single woman with no children, at the time, I did not understand the dynamics of becoming a blended family. The arrival of Peyton opened my eyes.

His sisters doted on this young man. I am envious of the bond that they share at times. Their bond has truly been a blessing, especially when life threw us lemons. His sisters helped us make lemonade along with another special lady, their mother and my ex-husband's first wife.

March 2011, Peyton was three-months-old. My ex-husband's first wife called me and asked if Peyton was coming over that Saturday? I laughed and thought it was a joke. I was thinking, "Not says the girl that I thought hated me, but she loves my baby." I asked, "Are you serious?" She replied, "Yes." I knew she was serious because her daughter was crazy about Peyton. I said, "You don't know Peyton, and he doesn't like anybody trying to say no nicely." She rebuked my answer and said, "Oh honey, yes he does know me." This special lady informed me that she had pictures in her phone to prove me wrong. I asked, "When did this all happen?" She said, "Peyton comes over every Saturday for hours."

I was oblivious to this! My ex-husband kept asking his first ex-wife to come to the car to see his son. She was thinking to herself, I don't want to see a baby that you have with your new wife. I could care less. But, she finally went to the care to see Peyton because her daughter had been showing her photos of him. This special lady did not want to be rude to her own baby, who was so happy to have a little brother.

The first ex-wife arrived at the car and fell in love with Peyton's eyes the moment he looked up at her. She said that he was so handsome, and took him out of the car seat. You can say that the rest is history. Peyton is her son, also. She had been keeping him on each Saturday while her daughter and ex-husband hung out together.

Our ex-husband would say to her, "You better not let anything happen to my baby or else." This special lady and our ex-husband became better friends because of Peyton. She has been a lifesaver for our families, in the past years and remains active in in the present day. My grandmother calls her Peyton's other mother. The bond that she and Peyton share is unbreakable. She also tried to save my marriage to her first husband, but couldn't sustain our marriage due to my husband's extra marital affair.

In the years to come, this special lady has been my backbone regarding Mr. Peyton Kameron Crawford (our son). Her family accepts him as her son. Blood could not make their bond any closer. She and I referred to each other jokingly as baby mama and baby daddy. It has taken us years to build this bond to raise our son, but I would not trade the journey or bond.

I loss three of my grandparents in 2016, and this special lady was there to care for Peyton and allow me time to grieve. She is one of very few people that I allowed to keep Peyton during work hours or personal travel. She means the world to me. Being a motherless and fatherless child, I could not have made it through many cries without her love and support for Peyton.

I thank God every day for my guardian angel, my friend, and my bonus daughters. My bonus daughters have also been very active in Peyton's life. They have traveled far and near for all his life's milestones, and even taken him on family vacations. Peyton and I are thankful and blessed.

Single moms, I would like to encourage you to find helpful scriptures that will help keep you with a calm spirit despite the storm. And, ones that will help you dance and make lemonade.

Passion Bragg

As I lay on the cold examination room table at The Health Care Group for Women at Missouri Baptist getting an annual well woman exam and thinking about my return to Mizzou, both was interrupted by a knock at the door. I heard a female voice, which was that of the medical assistant, saying, "Doctor, Here are Rolanda's results for your review." In my mind, this is a code for something doesn't look right. You need to see this now.

The examining gynecologist reviewed the documents, then said, "Okay Rolanda. Everything looks good; however, when did you say you had your last period?"

I go on to tell her my last menstrual cycle.

Then she says, "Your urine test came back negative, but the blood test shows you could be with child."

I sat straight up and said, "Doctor, I have never missed my period."

Then she said, "I'm going to send you for a pregnancy ultrasound today so we can be positive. The ultrasound department is right down the hall. Get dressed, pick up the ultrasound referral form from the front desk, and then head on over there. I will meet you there."

I followed the doctor's order. Once in the waiting area, I sat nervously for someone to call my name about the pregnancy ultrasound. Racing thoughts started completely taking over my mind. I started daydreaming about being pregnant and how my life would change. Even worse, how am I going to announce a pregnancy to my family, and more so my mother?

The ultrasound technician, who entered the waiting room and called my name, "Crews", interrupted my thoughts. I looked up, stood up, and replied all at once.

She asked me to follow her into an examination room filled with monitors, where she instructed me to get undressed. The technician informed me that the gynecologist would be in to assist her with the ultrasound, and then she left the room.

I got undressed, and then draped the thin gown over my naked body before hopping onto the examination table. Moments later, there was a knock at the examination room door, then my gynecologist entered the room.

The gynecologist started explaining the process while getting this blue gel to put on my abdomen. She proceeded to squeeze the gel and place it on my belly. Oh my God, it was so cold. She used an ultrasound wand to look at the inside of my abdomen and to see things better. During the process, she pressed down and circulated the wand all over my abdomen area. The gynecologist says, "Yes, Rolanda there is a life growing inside your belly." Then she called for her colleague to confirm the pregnancy, what she was currently seeing on the monitor before turning to me and stating, "It looks like you are around 5-months, exactly 23-weeks. Would you like to know the sex?"

At this point I was in complete shock, not only am I pregnant but I am five months along. I declined to know because I had it made up in my mind a baby was not in my future, and my next stop would be the corner of Forest Park Avenue and Boyle Avenue. If you are not from St. Louis, MO, I was going to push past the protestors at Planned Parenthood.

A week later, unknown to anyone, I returned to St. Louis from Mizzou, only to be devastated by the staff at Planned Parenthood. They explained I was too high risk for an abortion, and they would not be able to service me. Then I traveled to Hope Clinic for Women in Granite City, IL (across the bridge) expecting a different result, only to be told that they did not have an available appointment. And, by the next appointment time, I would be too far along for the procedure.

I remember breaking down, and telling the receptionist all I had been through. She then told me to try this place in Chicago. As I left Hope Clinic for Women, I started immediately scheduling an appointment and making arrangements to travel to Chicago the following week.

Guess what? I arrived at the clinic in Chicago, and the receptionist explained that my biparietal diameter (BPD) exceeded their requirements to perform the procedure. By now, you know I felt defeated and pissed. I was so confused as to why would they have me come all this way only to turn me around.

The receptionist stated that every ultrasound machine was different and each varied by two-weeks. And, unfortunately, they would have to turn me away. Then, she informed me of a place in Kansas that performed late-term procedures.

I walked to the parking lot crying my eyes out. I was exhausted and decided to check into a hotel for the night. Of course, I checked in with my fake identification card. Once settled, I called the clinic in Kansas.

The person on the other end of the phone said that the type of late-term procedure I was inquiring about would cost me a minimum of $4,000, and I would have to have the procedure within the next seven days.

I hung up the phone and began to come up with ways I could clear another $3,000 in the next few days without selling a kidney or going to jail. As I thought it through, each idea came to a dead end and I began to cry myself to sleep.

Later, I was awakened by hotel security. He knocked at the door to tell me my vehicle had been vandalized. I realized this city is foreign to me; however, I had a cousin who resided there. So, I called her, told her what was going on, and where I was staying.

Not even ten minutes later, the hotel phone rung. I answered and there was a voice I know all too well. "Rolanda, Are you okay? Just come home. I know you are pregnant, and we will get through this together," says my mother.

Two months later, on July 24, 2003, I welcomed my baby girl into the world at 19-years-old. What I thought was the end of my world, only proved to be the beginning.

Now 16 years later, I can't imagine my life without my only child, a.k.a. my blessing and my lesson. She not only saved me, she has shaped me into the woman and mother I am today.

Spending the latter part of my childhood and teenage years on the west side of St. Louis, 5500 block of Etzel, which I thought was the roughest hood to be apart of, I was seriously mistaken. It could have never prepared me for the real hoods that awaited me: adulthood and motherhood.

As my daughter and I began to grow up together, I knew I didn't want her to experience many of the hardships I had become all too familiar with at that point in my life. I knew as a mother, I wanted the best for her at any cost. There were places I could no longer frequent, there were people I knew for sure I wouldn't want in the company of my child, and there were things I just could no longer be apart of.

Parenting to me is the equivalent to building a house. You have to lay the foundation. That's a very important part.

Remember when you would hear an elder say, "Train up a child in the way he should go? And, when he is old, he will not depart from it." What if I told you that saying still holds, speaking from my own life. The foundation has to be solid. It has to be built on morals, values, and principles to withstand the storms of life.

As a black mother, I have taught and will continue to teach my daughter to stand in her truth and be grounded in her values. To own who she is and who she is destined to be.

There have been times when I didn't set the example for my child (don't act like you are perfect we have all done things we aren't proud of). I would say to her, "Be better than your mother. Nonetheless, if you fall short in any way, never make excuses. Be accountable for your actions, stand on your shortcomings, and reach your goals. Whatever you do remember FAILURE IS NOT AN OPTION. Show humility. It's received well by others. Reinvent yourself, multiple times if you have to. You can become whoever you desire to be."

As a parent remember, no one will ever be perfect, except when our children lay asleep in bed. They are our perfect little angels, then they wake up and all hell breaks loose, well at least that's been my experience.

I have had quite a few jobs in my life; however, becoming a mother is perhaps one of the most challenging obstacles I have ever come up against. But, it is truly the most rewarding. There is no manual. There are no off days. A mother's job is never done.

As a mother, we have to protect our children; provide for them, regardless of who else doesn't; be selfless; and be loving even when we sometimes don't love ourselves. We have to be our child's friend along with setting boundaries as their parent. We sacrifice our wants and needs for those of our children. We give advice. We do all of this with one goal in mind, to prepare our children for the world by equipping them with values, knowledge, and the skills to be productive citizens and good people.

Rolanda Crews

10 THE STEPMOM

How many 29-years-old stepmoms do you know? I don't know many. But, that's my story. I am Sway, a new wife, a first-time mom and a stepmom of four.

Being a wife and a stepmom happened all at one time. Some would say that it's a lot to handle. I say that it whips me into shape, and helps me gain a new role and understand my parenting journey.

My husband has three daughters and two sons, who were born prior to our marriage. Together he and I have a beautiful baby girl that we call Co-Co.

Our blended family has unique concerns, personalities, and dynamics. Every single child's personality is different, which I enjoy. There is a loud one, a very active one, a shy one, a sweet one with an attitude, and a very busy infant. Even their interactions with each other and us are different.

I do not look for our children by other mom's to call me mom at all. I'm cool with them referring to me by my first name, Swayze or Sway. Mom is a title that many hold closely, and I understand and know my place. I'm not their mother. I am a second mother

I feel like being a stepmom comes with certain rules and boundaries, which I am wise not to cross. I've been placed in my stepchildren lives as a second mother to help in anyway that I can, especially with how to become the best version of themselves. I believe that I'm here as another role model to guide them.

The conversations I have with them are different than the ones they have with their biological parents. That's expected.

I'm there for things like school activities, and to escape or avoid punishment with dad and to get their phones back. The children and I make plans that don't always work, but at least we can say that we tried.

I don't interfere with their moms' disciplinary actions because I don't feel like it's my place. Their moms communicate with my husband about picking the children up and taking them places, which I don't have a problem with.

Even having conversations with my husband is different. Sometimes he tells the children, "No." And, I have no clue about their conversations so I tell them, "Yes." I continue with my response because I never want to disappoint a child. My husband and I don't have disagreements about what I can do for the children.

I try my best to encourage everyone, the children, to be their best. I don't overwhelm them or get in their spaces. They and I are learning about each other and the rules for being a good stepmom.

I know what they like. One kid gets nuggets with bbq and sweet and sour sauce and a sprite, and another one loves cookies and will ask for them or say, "I don't care what I eat. I'm hungry." If my husband and I give them two options, my husband usually already knows exactly what they want and what to get.

I know when my husband is getting on the kids nerves. I can say for them, "You're irritating me." And, they laugh because it's how they feel.

I've asked others who are stepparents about their relationships with their stepchildren. Some have stated, "It takes time." Others say that when families are co-parenting and household do not operate the same; you have to figure out how to train a kid up to be balanced so everyone is respected.

I know as long as I'm married to this man the children are my responsibility. But, as a new step mom at times, I have wondered if the moms could be teaching different morals and values from what we exercise in our home. Then there are times that I may be overthinking the situation.

I've been told, "Don't tell me what to do." This is after my husband has informed me to tell them to get in the car. There are times that I am talking to them and being looked at like I'm crazy. When I address the situation with my husband, he doesn't see where my frustration is coming from. It's like he throws everything under a rug.

It puts me in a space where I don't want to be bothered and it makes me think that adding a new addition to our family is a problem. Once I told my husband that I would separate myself from it all. And, that I would not keep getting disrespected and that he's not doing enough to protect my feelings. It can be hard at times and you want to have the biggest support from your husband to make sure everything is good.

As a unit we are all learning each and every day. I love my blended family.

Swayze Polk

11 THE BATTLING DEPRESSION MOM

I struggle with how to start, where to start and even what to say. I knew I had a lot to share, especially for flawed moms. Getting it right is sometimes getting it wrong more often.

When I had my son there where so many questions. Although I was humbled in my spirit, I knew I was going to be a great mother. As most of us know, we had to be mothers before our time. It happened at some point in our childhood.

As a young girl, eight-years-old is the earliest I can recall, I was Momma Rida. The parenting load got heavier as I got older.

My mother was a solid person in her children's lives. She gave us all of the essentials we needed, such as clothes, food, roof over our heads, and a load of access to being outside playing. LOL. Every child loved this back then. In our home, I was the one doing most of the work, preparing dinner, cleaning the house, combing hair (my mom was not the best hairdresser at that time, so ponytails and braids it was, LOL), and getting my siblings and me ready for school. Then I had to do it all over again when we can home.

I was the keeper of my siblings, and even my mother at some point in time, that story is for another book. So, yes, being a mom was actually easy, second nature.

While my son was still a newborn, I had major support from my mother and his father's mother. Taking breaks and getting sleep were a plus at times, but not much as I would have liked. Now, I know you're thinking, where was his father? His father was very much so solid in our son's life. There has never been a question mark placed in that area. He and I lived in two different states.

Living separately while parenting became a stress point for me and at that time, I was unaware of what was happening. My son's father could not offer emotional and social support the way that I needed it after having the baby. I needed him to fill a void, make sure things were done properly.

My son and I traveled back and forth from time to time to visit his father. The visits were important so we could continue to bond and grow. But, it wasn't much, due to other circumstances such as a mix of physical, emotional, and behavioral changes associated with having a baby and I was doing everything on my own.

Thinking back on those times, I thought things started to come together for me when my son turned two-years-old. This is me thinking about events that happened 10 years ago, and not now. I was bringing stability to my life, feeling grounded, and moving in the right direction. Therefore, I was able to focus on achieving life stability. What was going to be my next step? How was I going to make something out of my life? These are the questions that helped me start to make many plans and arrangements that I knew were right strides.

Though I was not fully stable, I wasn't fully committed to anything. Keep in mind, I was in major depression at this time and didn't know the signs, symptoms, or causes of depression and how it could impact everything I do in my daily life. However, I always was a mother and put my son first. There was never a thought neglect him.

At 17 to 25-years-old, I started experiencing life in a way that I had never been able to before. It was during that time that I had begun dating my son's father and facing my first real relationship. I was serious about mastering love and placing all of my time, focus, energy into our relationship. I was ensuring value and importance, and doing the right things.

Although, through the mist of that, I was missing a major piece and that was placing myself first, loving myself that was in no way comparable to how someone else could love me. Also, truly focusing and analyzing who I was and were my life was going.

Keep in mind that the frontal lobe of our brains, which allows us to make logical and strategic discussion, isn't fully developed until 25-years-old. Not to say that was an excuse for anything that I'd done.

I was just trying to figure out everything the best way that I could. Now, I had people that gave me great advice, but due to the oversight of my emotional state and well being, that information did not resonate with me, as it should've.

By that time, my son was turning five-years-old. And, as his mother, I was still solid being a caretaker, a nurturer, a supporter, a provider, a nurse, a counselor, an educator, and a playmate to him. Every single mom duty that is required while alone with your child during parenting time. LOL. And, the list goes on and on. Though there are challenges with being a single mom, I won't complain. I was being, and still I am everything my son needs and more.

Now that my son was becoming self-sufficient and no one had a problem with babysitting him, I began hanging out with friends, partying, and traveling. I was enjoying my many trips to Miami. It's a place for having fun, but not living for me.

During this period, I was in depression, although I didn't know what it felt like or the symptoms and warning signs. This was the part where my life started to take a major turn, and too quickly for me to grab hold of it or evaluate what was happening.

I started to feel sad all the time, and wanted to be isolated most of the time. The sadness wouldn't allow me to be alone. I thought the sadness was due to a lack of mental support from my son's father. I cannot stress enough that my son's father was a great provider to him. My son did and does not want for anything.

I didn't know the difference between sadness and depression. And, didn't realize help was needed so I continued living my best life, as we call it. But, honestly, I was living my best lie. I thought my life was meaningful and fulfilling, which it was for other people who could see my life from the outside.

I was making someone else happy everyday. My friends were benefiting the most because I was everything to them that I should been to myself-supportive, encouraging, a friend, honest, loving, forgiving, mindful, trustworthy, a motivator, and a believer. I was focusing externally instead of internally, and was starting to drink, party, and travel way too much.

I encountered toxic relationships with male friends, which was dangerous for my mental health, but again I didn't know that at the time. No, I was not abused or mistreated in anyway by male friends. In fact, the men I dated really wanted to play a major role in my life. However, I was not able to reciprocate in the relationship. I was not able to continue to nurture feelings the same way that someone else did to me. I had to figure out how to show regard for my own well-being and happiness.

As a result, I turned my dating situations into something that became hurtful. The best way to describe what I was experiencing, I had to take a look at myself outside of being a mom, a partner in a relationship, and a friend and internalize the emotions I had been feeling through that change.

Once my son was placed to bed, and well taken care of it was my time to not be alone with my thoughts and emotional self. I went out with friends, and sometimes by myself to meet new people.

During this time, I tried to drink and dance my problems away. I addressed my problems with changes in my hairstyles, and purchases. I ran my credit cards up, and credit score down. I thought a new dress would make everything better. I tried to keep busy and work my problems away, which made me sadder. Honestly, I tried to do everything I could think of, outside of taking my own life, consuming drugs or becoming an alcoholic, to get away from what I was feeling and running from.

In this part of my life, I wasn't being my greatest support, my strongest motivation, and my biggest comfort to myself the way I was to others. My depression only becomes worse when someone informed me of the harm and damage that I was causing myself. The person was helping me to see things outside of my own lens, and to bring all of this to an immediate and abrupt stop.

Once I realized what had taken place and how I had gotten so far from who I was, I dug deeper into my childhood and the things that caused me pain to deal with and face depression- all of the choices that I made to this point. I began to think about the people that hurt me, the overexposed and underprepared impact on children's learning and behavior, and growing up in poverty and the impact it has on a person.

I went into hibernation, a deeper, darker depression. No one, I mean no one, knew what I was experiencing. Again, others were looking at the external of who I was and believing I had the best life, no worries, no complaints, and no real struggles.

Imagine me in this horrific mental state of depression and still being mommy, super mom. Yes, I'll give myself a pat on the back for this involvement.

I have faced my darkest hours of life. I almost lost my home, was buried in debt, and had my car repossessed. It was hard to go through this and come out even stronger than what I was when I entered motherhood and depression.

I know you are wonder if I sought out professional help. No, I did not. And, yes, I do believe in getting professional help for depression. This was a journey that I needed to experience with myself and alone to grasp the full understanding of why I went through all that I went through. It was very personal to me. I needed every quiet and isolated moment that to give myself full clarity of each moment and experience, and to evaluate the next journey in my life of being my greatest source of achievement and inspiration.

Here we are, my son is almost 12-years-old. I have shared some of what I experienced with him. The rest of my experience will be told to him on another date, at a later time. I wanted my son to know depression is real and difficult to deal with, and he has more control over his feelings than he realize. He has to recognize his feelings and take positive steps to find himself and do things that make him feel good.

Feeling something you cannot quite explain makes it difficult to reach out to someone for help. However, you must push through and get support. For me, staying connected and taking part social activities with friends made a big difference in how I was coping with my depression, and becoming who I was supposed to be.

Now, I'm addressing all the things that made me feel bruised and broken, starting my own business, and working toward my master's degree and expecting to graduate fall 2020. Too, I'm starting the home buying process.

More importantly, I have become a professional speaker, and a voice and a life coach. Always, I have had a passion to serve and be of service, especially in the areas of self-development, and help other people reach and become their greatest self. I'm able to fulfill myself personally and follow my inner passion because I was able to face myself, my own worst enemy.

No matter how or where life takes us, we have to be aware of depression and learn the causes, symptoms, treatments, and how to cope with it. At all times, we must be our greatest and biggest supporter, step into our passion, purpose, and power, and believe what The Most High has for you is for you.

As mothers, we face many challenges and bear many burdens. Yet, The Most High honors mothers. Don't be ashamed or guilty of your experience as a mother. Learn about support groups and services that are just for mothers. Surround yourself with people who inspire, acknowledge, and accept you working through your feelings.

I am not the only mother who has experienced what depression feels like, hell on earth. Though, I know we are the creators of our hell and our heaven in our current existence.

Today, I live in my heaven. Today, I live for me. Today, I am the greatest Sherida L. Williams, who helps other individuals, build communities, and educate to create new knowledge.

I want to acknowledge people in my life, although I won't list names, and speak my appreciation. It is habit for me to tell people what I love and appreciate about them. Always, I say, "Thank you." I am mindful to let them know they matter in the moment and when it counts the most.

People in my life deserve to be recognized and are equally valued. Usually, I can't tell if they are in my life for a reason, season or lifetime. Whichever, I am grateful for everyone's presence to help me grow and learn, and navigate life's challenges.

What I thought was the worst time of my life actually was the best. The time was an opportunity for me to reach my own potential and build better mental health, a state of well-being.

I am no longer at the lowest and hardest time. I can honestly say, "I love myself," which has given me the ability to believe in myself with confidence, and to effectively give love and guidance to others.

I am thankful for my new experiences and new ways to achieve my goals in life. I continue to speak my truth, and believe in myself.

In closing, I'm open and honest about my depression. I'm willing to have conversations and let you know there is hope. Depression can be prevented and treated.

If there is help, guidance, and strong support, there are no limits to your greatness. When you eliminate your why, you gain your what, how, and when!

Sherida L. Williams

Amber Farrar

CLOSING LETTERS

To the Single Mom,

    Do you believe in fairy tales? Do you remember being a kid, dreaming about meeting your Prince Charming, falling in love, getting married, and having kids, a dog, and a big house with a 2-car garage and a white picket fence? Basically, living the American Dream.

    Like many little girls, I wanted to be Cinderella or a princess in a movie. And, like many adult women, I lived in illusion.

    I believe all women give some thought to what would my dream life look like and what are ways to start living my dream life?

    We live in illusion of things, and believe we were born into this world where everything should be this way or that way. In reality, the world is what you make of it.

    You have to learn how to play the hand you were dealt. Who determines a perfect hand? You do! Believe the hand you've been given is perfect enough for you. Even with what seems like the worst hand, you can create and live your best life.

    I must admit that I was one of those girls who believed in the fairytale life. And, put my all into a situation. My reality was an illusion, not my perfect world.

    I was dealing with emotional abuse that many women face in relationships: cheating, screaming, fighting and arguing; and lies, disrespect, and breakups to makeup. All of this for what I thought was mine.

    What was really happening? Again, my reality was an illusion. Which meant my love was an illusion.

    Eleven years later, after all the sweat and tears that I

put into loving what I thought was perfect for me, I have two kids and a dog. My kids have a broken and traumatized mother. So with that being said, wasted time is worse than wasted money became my reality.

So, who is to blame? Is it me or it is my mother? Describing me is so close to describer her. Can trauma be passed on? Can I pass my trauma to my children?

Now that I know trauma has been passed through generations, I have a willingness and amazing opportunity to give my children everything possible they need for the best start in life, provide them with a life better than mine. I can do this, and you can do this.

The old adage "time heals all wounds" may have some truth to it, but it is no cure for trauma. Trauma, in some cases, brings on feelings of hopelessness and helplessness that interferes with growing and learning in every aspect of life. Can trauma be healed?

We expose our children to our trauma and depression. They see our tears, anger, disconnection, isolation, and brokenness, same experiences we saw manifest across multiple generations in our families. We must show our children how to heal and move on.

Yes, it is easier said than done. So when and how do we break the cycle? Now is the time for us to learn about emotional and psychological trauma, including the types, co-occurring disorders, causes and risk factors, signs and symptoms, and effects. We live in the present, and not in feelings of the past.

Dealing with disappointment from what we thought would be the best life is healing, if done on our own or with professional therapy and counseling. Acknowledging and accepting how deep hurts within us takes effort on our part because we've been wounded deeply, and sometimes the wound is embedded in our soul. Blocking it out, overlooking it, and staying quiet won't help us.

No matter how you avoid it, dress it up, or lie about it, your truth is still yours. Take it and learn from it. Your story is your story because you are uniquely you.

Don't be ashamed of what you've experienced, been through. Those hurdles you got over can help someone else struggling with the same issues. We have to understand that it's okay to not be okay.

Buying your kids material things, taking them on trips, and teaching them certain things make them superior to others are superficial changes to disguise what's happening, what's going on. Let's all agree to start with each other, and teach and show our children what it means to be empathetic and compassionate. They have a right to see, without glasses, what it looks like to be happy.

Happiness is an inside job. So work on yourself. Let your children inherit happiness, not trauma, depression, and brokenness.

I read an article, which implied, broken parents raise broken children, send them to broken schools with broken teachers in broken communities, and patrolled by broken officers. We're all broken and need to heal! Let's break the cycle.

Mahoganie Bryant

To the Breastfeeding Mom,

    I know you thought after giving birth to your baby, you would finally have control over your body again. Wrong! Your new little perfect baby now has even more control.

    You can't make a move without questioning yourself. Did I pump enough milk for my baby? When was the last time I nursed my baby? Looking at the clock, when is the next time I have to nurse my baby? How will I know if my baby is getting enough milk? And, the common breastfeeding questions go on and on.

    Take on breastfeeding with confidence. Natural instincts don't just happen. Address your baby's needs, and feed as often as you need. Be informed, and avoid breastfeeding myths. And, surround yourself with support. There are people who want you to succeed with breastfeeding.

    The benefits of breastfeeding for baby and mom are rewarding. The baby has the best nutrients possible, and less risk of diseases, infections, and other health issues in childhood and later in life. The mom has the best health as well, and closeness with her baby.

    Follow the natural flow of life. It doesn't matter if you decide to breastfeed your baby for two weeks or two years, the milk your body produces is made especially for your baby.

    Some days, you will feel breastfeeding is emotionally and physically draining. Making sure you produce enough milk will always be your biggest concern and burden, but worrying and stressing reduces your milk supply. Embracing breastfeeding as a gift, not a sacrifice, will help you triumph.

It is mind over matter. You can provide enough milk for your baby if you believe you can. When you pump, try to be as relaxed as possible with a clear mind.

I love affirmations for encouragement and reminders. Always, tell yourself your body was made for breastfeeding, and it will produce enough milk for your baby.

Also, be organized. Create a pumping and feeding schedule that works for you.

To me, breastfeeding is one of the most rewarding parts of motherhood. When I nurse my precious baby and she looks into my eyes as she sucks the life out of me, she and I both are creating a bond in an amazing and indescribable way.

Just think about it, you've carried a baby and protected him or her in the womb for nine long months. And, now, your body has continued to give them nutrients and antibodies to improve in relation to survival, health, and development.

Try to breastfeed for as long as you can, and never feel bad if you can't keep up or if it can't integrate it into your work life or lifestyle.

If you're a stay at home mom, who just can't produce enough or a working mom, who can't find the time to pump, never beat yourself up. Supplementing with formula is okay. The most important outcome is to have a happy, healthy baby.

As flawed moms, our breastfeeding and mothering journey will never be perfect, or go as planned. In order to take care of your baby, you have to practice self-care, take care of yourself emotionally and physically.

You may never desire to breastfeed, or love the

experience for years and with each of your babies. Whatever you choose, just be the best mom you can be. Embrace your flaws. Your baby sees the little imperfections and feels the greatest love.

Demi Owens

P.S. Below I've added a few tips for you to make breastfeeding a little easier:

- INVEST. You need a good electric pump (check with your insurance first, most provide free pumps) and postnatal vitamins they will supply your body with everything your baby is taking and keep your energy up.
- HYDRATE. You will always be thirsty.
- EAT CLEAN. Your diet is your babies diet.
- PUMP EVERY 2 HOURS. This is important so you get the required pumps in per day. It will keep your body producing more and more milk for your baby.
- STOCK YOUR FREEZER. When storing milk, store 4oz and 6oz bags. This will put you ahead and help you prepare your return to work and baby's development.
- STAY CONSISTENT. The moment your body doesn't think you need milk it will stop producing.
- BE PROUD. Your body is literally making liquid gold!

Dear Flawed Moms,

Thank you for allowing me to pour courage and confidence into you. My growing and learning allow me to reflect as far back as I can recall and today affirm my best is yet to come. I hope my book, Flawed Mom Too, encourages you to check-in with yourself. You are amazing remember that. Choose to:

Be prepared. Be aware of your surroundings and whomever you roll with. Be sure whoever got you, got you! Love everyone who comes into your presence, yet focus closely on the people who focus on you. Life is too short to be concerned with other people issues or to worry, try to understand situations not meant to be understood by you.

Stop accumulating stuff and begin learning to take out the trash (other's issue and negativity). Know you deserve better and your time is valuable, and you can waste so much of your valuable time trying to fix other people lives. Believe everything is not repairable. Give your battles to our Heavenly Father. Work on you. Start all over and rebuild your life from scratch. Give yourself permission to make the rest of your life the best of your life. Be good to yourself so you can be good to others. Remember that when you are not mentally healthy or sound you are not any good to anyone, including yourself. Take good care of yourself, which is necessary to have a happy and productive life. Own up to your mistakes. Tell yourself you messed up, and then move on and be strong. Stand up for you and your beliefs. Be true to who you really are in order to be real with anyone else. Have self-respect. Accept your own self.

Nothing from my past holds anything I want today: to be sincere, open-minded and fair. I wish to continue taking care of myself through education, self-love, self-respect, proactive behavior, financial freedom, and good health.

My past does not define who I am today, it has molded me into a fierce yet beautiful being.

Take care, with love,
Flawed Mom, Amber Farrar

Made in the
USA
Columbia, SC